ATLANTIC STUDIES ON SOCIETY IN CHANGE
No. 55

Editor-in-Chief Béla K. Király
Associate Editor-in-Chief Peter Pastor

CHRISTIANS, JEWS AND OTHER WORLDS

Patterns of Conflict and Accomodation

The Avery Lectures in History

Edited by Philip F. Gallagher

UNIVERSITY
PRESS OF
AMERICA

Lanham • New York • London

Copyright © 1988 by

University Press of America,® Inc.

4720 Boston Way
Lanham, MD 20706

3 Henrietta Street
London WC2E 8LU England

British Cataloging in Publication Information Available

Co-published by arrangement with
Atlantic Research and Publications, Inc.

Library of Congress Cataloging-in-Publication Data

Christians, Jews, and other worlds.

(Atlantic studies on society in change ; no. 55)
Includes index.
1. Christianity and other religions—History.
I. Gallagher, Philip F. II. Series.
BR127.C4744   1988   261.2'09   88–89
ISBN 0–8191–6894–7 (alk. paper)

For

THEODORE M. AVERY JR.

Student and Friend

of the Department of History

TABLE OF CONTENTS

PREFACE

The Avery Lectures in History were created to stimulate thinking and discussion about the importance of cultural context where faiths and people of different faiths confront one another. The title of the published version of the talks, *Christians, Jews and Other Worlds: Patterns of Conflict and Accommodation*, is only descriptive since no single thesis emerged from the papers presented.

The essays do not appear in the order in which they were given, nor is their ordering based on simple chronology. The first three treat matters of specific concern to Christians and Jews since the sixteenth century. The last two examine the broad cultural contexts within which Christians, with vastly different goals in mind, confronted the Turks in the fourteenth and fifteenth and the Chinese in the sixteenth and seventeenth centuries.

In "Toward an Understanding of Luther's Attacks on the Jews," Mark U. Edwards Jr. asks those concerned with Martin Luther and his theology to study more thoroughly his anti-Jewish writings. While they have been interpreted by some as the product of Luther's old age and declining health, others have rejected them out of hand. Edwards advocates examining these tracts in their fullest historical context "to see what produced them and whether anything might be learned from them."

Edwards concludes that Luther's vitriolic attacks on the Jews were not aberrations to be associated with senility, but "fit into a larger Augustinian and apocalyptic world-view that Luther applied consistently to all of his opponents." Luther believed all of his opponents—whether Catholics, Jews or "fanatics"—were blasphemers against God and hence a risk to the community; thus, they deserved whatever attack they received. Lastly, Edwards suggests that Luther's major target was not the Jews themselves, but rather Rabbinic

IX

exegesis which clashed so strikingly with traditional Christian exegesis.

Our second paper seeks to understand why Lutherans were slow to develop a coherent social policy in response to problems created by industrialization and urbanization in nineteenth- and twentieth-century Germany. In "The German Protestant Social Dilemma: from Bismarck to Hitler," William O. Shanahan suggests that understanding must be rooted in a long series of complex considerations. Among these were the traditionally close ties between the German state(s) and the consistently conservative Evangelical-Protestant Lutheran churches, as well as their persistent emphasis on doctrine and theology with its rejection of humanism and doctrines of "progress." Nor can one overlook the remarkable degree to which, in the late nineteenth and twentieth centuries, the churches came to identify and justify theological orthodoxy and their self interests with nationalism, the monarchy, and the social order prior to World War I.

Although notable, sometimes heroic, efforts to face the social question took place, they never matured. By the late 1920s, Evangelical-Protestant leaders, yielding to theologically based conservative tendencies, rejected parliamentary democracy and threw their support to those who opposed the Weimar republic. Shanahan's analysis underlines the importance of the role of Lutheran theology, especially its teaching on church and state, in these developments.

With John Murray Cuddihy's contribution we encounter a sociologist reflecting on the Holocaust or, in the author's words, reflecting on debates about the Holocaust. "I am speaking about speech about the Holocaust; I am talking about Holocaust ideologies.... Historiography, not history." Cuddihy does not expect his readers to remain indifferent to his frank reflections.

Cuddihy entitles his article "The Holocaust: the Latent Issue in the Uniqueness Debate." He begins by surveying the prominent participants in the debate and by summarizing their arguments for and against the claim that the Holocaust was a unique historical event. For some the Holocaust is unique because it was directed by definition against the Jews and is thus reducible to anti-Semitism; for others, the Holocaust was not only anti-Semitic, it was anti-Christian and anti-human.

But historical judgment on the uniqueness claim is not
Cuddihy's major interest. "My chief interest in the uniqueness claim is to ask: What, today, is the Jewish community
getting out of this claim? What function is the consuming
interest in the Holocaust performing for the Jewish subculture and its members?" He then proceeds to a functional
analysis which comes before "the profane eyes of a sociologist." Not everyone will agree with his analysis; few will miss
his point.

Our fourth offering is Anthony Luttrell's "The Hospitallers
of Rhodes Confront the Turks: 1306-1421." The Latin military order known as the Order of the Hospital of St. John
of Jerusalem or the Hospitallers traces its origins to the period
after the First Crusade. Luttrell is concerned here with the
order's *raison d'être* and activity at a time when the crusades were finished. What were the Hospitallers' long-range
goals; how did they relate to the plans of the Papacy, to the
defense of Constantinople, to the commercial adventurers
of the Italian maritime cities, and to the Turkic peoples
they faced from their offshore headquarters on the island
of Rhodes which they had conquered between 1306 and 1310?

Luttrell catalogues the remarkable manner in which
the Hospitallers managed not only to stave off the destruction which befell the Templars and appropriate to themselves the income of the fallen order, but also to contain the
Turks and keep alive an evolving role in a complex, confused
political and religious environment.

Did Christian doctrine and religious feeling play a major
role in determining the policy and strategy of the Hospitallers?
Luttrell tells us that they never forgot "they were Latin
Christians and members of a religious order...established...
to oppose the Turks." He also points out that while they
successfully defended Rhodes and provided a measure of
security to the Aegean, they probably did so by being prag-
matic: whether their conflicts were with the Turks, the Latin
mercantile republics, or the schismatic Christians of Byzantium, they avoided overextending themselves, they kept
themselves under control, they avoided extremes. Theology
and doctrine played a smaller role here than in Lutheran
Europe.

In our final essay Charlton M. Lewis explains how Jesuit

missionaries in the late sixteenth and early seventeenth centuries mixed Christianity with the most progressive elements of Renaissance intellectual life to convince about 70,000 Chinese to be baptized Christians by 1640. His article is entitled "Christianity and Science in Late Ming China: Jesuit Missionaries and the Conversion of the Literati."

His paper not only deals with the metamorphosis that Christianity underwent in an effort to adjust to Chinese sensibilities, but also explores "the ways in which Jesuit teachings on Christianity and science fitted into the mental world of the Chinese educated elite in the late Ming period." This short study of "the experience of Christianity in the Chinese world helps us to appreciate the importance of cultural context for all religions in all times and places. It also helps us to understand how ideas change their meanings as they move from one human environment to another."

There are a number of persons whose generous help in bringing these essays to the point of publication must be noted. The History Department is most grateful to Theodore M. Avery Jr. whose generous financial contribution made the series and its publication possible. Professors Christoph M. Kimmich and Paula S. Fichtner, as former chairs of the History Department, helped in recruiting our speakers, as did Professors Teofilo Ruiz and Donald F. M. Gerardi, the latter in his capacity as Director of the Religious Studies Program. The Brooklyn College Humanities Institute, through the work of its Director, Professor Robert J. Viscusi, and Louis S. Asekoff, co-sponsored the series and provided us with much logistical support; we are very grateful to them. Above all I must thank Professor Paula Fichtner for her critical reading and frequent advice in bringing this project to its present point. Lastly, I am grateful to Carol Green, my secretary for this publication, for typing the entire manuscript and making me aware of things I would otherwise have missed.

Brooklyn College
May 28, 1987

Philip F. Gallagher
Assistant Professor of History

TOWARD AN UNDERSTANDING OF LUTHER'S ATTACKS ON THE JEWS

Mark U. Edwards Jr. [1]

Shortly after the infamous *Kristalnacht* of 9-10 November 1938, which saw the systematic destruction of Jewish synagogues and property throughout Nazi Germany, the bishop of Thuringia, Martin Sasse, issued a tract that began:

> On 10 November 1938, on Luther's birthday, the synagogues in Germany are aflame. As atonement for the murder by Jewish hand of the embassy secretary von Rath, the power of the Jews in economic affairs in the New Germany is finally broken by the German people, and thus is capped the blessed struggle of our Leader for the complete liberation of our people. World Catholicism and Oxford World Protestantism along with the western democracies raise their voices as protectors of the Jews against the Third Reich's opposition to the Jews. In this hour the voice must be heard of the man, who, as the German prophet in the sixteenth century, began, first out of ignorance as a friend of the Jews, /and/ who, driven by his conscience, driven by experience and reality, became the greatest anti-Semite of his time, the warner of his people against the Jews....

Sasse followed his introduction with excerpts from Luther's 1543 *On the Jews and Their Lies*, including a favorite in the anti-Semitic arsenal: Luther's harsh recommendations to secular authorities on how to deal with the Jews. According to Luther, their synagogues and schools should be burned and whatever would not burn should be buried. Their homes should be destroyed. All their prayer books and Talmudic writings should be taken from them. Their rabbis should be forbidden to teach. Their safe-conducts on highways should be revoked. Their usury should be forbidden, and their money taken from them. They should be put to work in the fields so that they earned their living by the sweat of their brows; better yet, they should be expelled after a portion of their wealth had been confiscated. It was, Luther said, the duty of the secular authorities to implement these recommendations and the duty of the ecclesiastical authorities to warn and instruct their congregations about the Jews and their lies.

This horrible little tract with the atrocities it was meant to justify poses for many who are concerned with Luther and his theology a most difficult question: how are they to interpret his anti-Jewish writings? If Luther were merely an obscure figure centuries dead, these writings could be easily dismissed. But Luther's teachings remain a potent force in Christian theology and German society to the present day, so his attacks on the Jews, especially in view of the Holocaust, cannot be ignored or rationalized away. In the years since World War II scholars of Luther have tended to take one of three tacks:

1. Some have attempted to explain the anti-Jewish writings as the unfortunate product of ill health and old age. This is a very convenient approach unless it can be shown, as I think it can, that this argument ignores too much of the historic record.

2. Others have decided, and this includes many avowedly Christian scholars, that they must simply condemn these writings as beyond defense and explanation. This, too, has its attractions, since it makes one's abhorrence of anti-Semitism unequivocally clear and divorces one from the anti-Semitic attitudes of past Christianity. If, however, as with the first option, it can be shown that Luther's attacks are an integral part of his theology, then a blanket condemnation runs the risk of rejecting *all* of Luther's theology, which most Christians would be unwilling to do.

3. Finally, some scholars, including myself, advocate studying these attacks within their historic context to see what produced them and whether anything might be learned from them. This is what I shall attempt to accomplish in

the rest of my presentation. Given a better understanding of Luther's attacks, we might still choose to ignore the attacks, to dismiss them as aberrations, or to condemn them out of hand, but our decision would be much better informed. Moreover, an historical examination may suggest other options we have not considered yet.

In examining the historical genesis and significance of Luther's attacks on the Jews, I wish to make four interrelated points.

1. These attacks are not aberrations. Their harshness is not unique; Luther attacked all his opponents with similar if not greater vitriol. They are not peculiar to his old age; he had always written passionately abusive attacks on opponents, and ill health and aging had at most exacerbated this longstanding characteristic.

2. The attacks fit into a larger Augustinian and apocalyptic world-view that Luther applied consistently to all of his opponents. He saw all of them — Catholics, Turks, "fanatic" Protestants, and Jews — as willing servants of Satan, and with even-handed vitriol he treated them accordingly.

3. Luther believed that Catholics, "fanatics," and Jews committed blasphemy against God. If rulers tolerated such blasphemy within their territories, Luther believed, they invited divine judgment against them and their people. So Luther called upon secular authorities to take drastic steps against the blasphemous activity of each of these groups.

4. The major target of Luther's anti-Jewish writings is not the Jews themselves, but rather Rabbinic exegesis. Rabbinic commentaries on the Hebrew bible challenged the traditional Christian exegesis that found trinitarian references and interpreted Messianic passages as referring to Jesus. Luther saw this challenge as a deadly danger, and so in the bulk of his anti-Jewish writings he sought to convince Protestant preachers, teachers, and exegetes to hew to the traditional Christian exegesis and to shun the Rabbinic alternative.

For those of you not familiar with Luther's life or his attacks on the Jews, let me offer a brief sketch. [2]

Martin Luther spent most of his adult life as a professor of Biblical theology at the University of Wittenberg. In 1517, at the age of 34, he became embroiled in a controversy over indulgences and papal authority. What started as an academic and theological dispute soon turned into a popular movement against the Roman Catholic church, the papacy, and traditional Catholic beliefs and practices. At the heart of his challenge, and the movement it engendered, was the conviction that salvation lay solely in God's gift rather than in man's action. This conviction may be conveniently summarized by the Pauline phrase: "justification by faith alone apart from works of the law." This was the rallying cry of nascent Protestantism.

Good works for Luther and his followers were, therefore, a consequence of justification rather than a condition for acquiring justification. Good works were a "fruit of faith." Accordingly, Luther attacked all Catholic teachings and practices that suggested that human beings could, in even the most tenuous sense, merit justification by what they did. In these attacks he took as his model and justification Jesus' criticism of the legalism of the Pharisees and St. Paul's rejection of justification through the observance of the law. Human beings were saved solely by Christ's death on the cross, Luther insisted. An individual need only have faith that Christ had died for him. And this faith itself was a gift of God.

This Lutheran rejection of "works righteousness" and "legalism" had from the beginning an anti-Jewish potential. The pharisaic Jew of the New Testament accounts was the prototype of the self-righteous human being who wished to earn his salvation apart from God. He was the archetypal sinner, estranged from God and deluded about his own abilities and goodness. Of course, Luther's understanding of the Gospel did not create this negative stereotype of the works-righteous Jew. To varying degrees throughout the history of Christianity into Luther's day, the Jew had been so characterized and attacked by Christians. [3]

Given this anti-Jewish potential, it is perhaps surprising that Luther's first treatise on the Jews was for the sixteenth century a remarkably mild and even friendly pamphlet. *That Jesus Christ Was a Born Jew*, published in 1523, was an avowedly missionary tract. [4] Its attacks were largely directed not at Jews but at the papacy and what Luther labeled "papists." Luther especially faulted the way the Jews had been treated by Christian society. In a remarkable passage Luther advocated a reversal of the customary treatment of the Jews:

> Therefore, I would request and advise that one manage them decently and instruct them from the Scripture so that some of them might be brought along. But since we now drive them with force and slander them, accuse them of having Christian blood if they don't stink, and who knows what other foolishness, so that they are regarded just as dogs—what good can we expect to accomplish with them? Similarly, that we forbid them to work, do business, and have other human association with us, so that we drive them to usury—how does that help them? If we wish to help them, we must practice on them not the papal law but rather the Christian law of love, and accept them in a friendly fashion, allowing them to work and make a living, so that they gain the reason and opportunity to be with and among us /and/ to see and to hear our Christian teaching and life. If some are obstinate, what does it matter? After all, we too are not all good Christians. Here I will let matters rest until I see what I have accomplished. [5]

Today we are made uneasy by even a "friendly" attempt at Christian mission among the Jews. But we should not let our contemporary sensibilities obscure the remarkable nature of this treatise for the sixteenth century. Certainly, Luther's Jewish contemporaries recognized that this was no ordinary appeal. We have, for example, reports of Jews circulating copies of the treatise throughout Europe.

It is the very mildness of this first treatise that makes the later attacks so striking. For a decade and a half Luther had little publicly to say about the Jews. Then, in 1538, he published *Against the Sabbatarians*, an attack on arguments Jews were allegedly using to gain Christian proselytes. [6] Five years later, in 1543, he issued three treatises against Jewish arguments, practices, and exegesis.

The most notorious of these treatises is *On the Jews and Their Lies*. It was written in response to a treatise (now apparently lost) in which a Jew, in dialogue with a Christian, attacked Jesus, the Virgin Mary, and Christian exegesis of the Hebrew Scripture. It is important to recognize that the bulk of Luther's treatise, and of its two companions, consisted of exegesis of the Hebrew Bible and a defense of a specifically Christian reading of these scriptures. Sustained attacks on the Jews themselves, apart from these exegetical issues, comprise only a small portion of these treatises. Yet it will surprise no one that the lengthy exegetical passages and the Christological arguments have long been forgotten, superseded in many cases by improvements in biblical scholarship, while the hostile recommendations for the treatment of the Jews have survived in fragmented form in the memories and writings of anti-Semites. Their favorite source has been the third section of *On the Jews and Their Lies*, in which Luther dealt with alleged Jewish slanders against the Virgin Mary and her son, Jesus. To give you an idea of the style and tone of Luther's argumentation, let me offer you some examples drawn from this treatise. I will concentrate on some of his anti-Jewish arguments, rather than on his exegetical opinions, because of the importance of these arguments for our deliberations.

Early in the treatise Luther took up and attempted to refute several claims and boasts allegedly made by the Jews. For example, the Jews were greatly conceited, Luther said, because God had spoken with them and given them the Law of Moses on Mount Sinai. Through the Law they had entered into a marriage with God and had become His bride. But it was apparent from the Old Testament histories that they had become a besmirched bride, an incorrigible whore and wicked slut with whom God continually had to scuffle. This applied not only to the wicked Jews of the past but also to the Jews of Luther's own day, because their fifteen-hundred-year exile and suffering proved that they were one with the whoring Jews described in the Old Testament and were not God's people. To have God's word meant nothing. The devils in hell had God's word. At issue was the fact that the Jews failed to keep God's word. Outward obedience to the Law of Moses, apart from obedience to the Ten Commandments, meant nothing. Moses himself was aware that no one could keep God's commandments except those whose sins God forgave. This required a man who bore our sins for us. It was of this man that Christians spoke and taught. It was of such a man that the prophets and apostles spoke and taught. [7] In the second section of the treatise Luther examined the conflicting interpretations of various prophetic texts in the Hebrew Scripture that Christians interpreted as referring to the Messiah and as proving this Messiah to be Jesus. But the Jews, Luther wrote, were so convinced that the Messiah had not yet come that even if all the angels and God Himself said otherwise, the Jews would not believe them. Much less were they willing to listen to Christian exegetes and even former Jews, although these exegetes had so mightily overcome the arguments of the Jews. "But their accursed rabbis, who know better indeed, so wantonly poison their poor youth and common people and turn them from the truth. For I believe that if such writings were read by the common man and the youth, they would stone all their rabbis and hate them worse than we Christians do." [8]

In the third section Luther dealt with alleged Jewish slanders against the Virgin Mary and her son, Jesus. It is from this section that anti-Semites have most often taken their quotes. Luther accused the Jews of claiming that Jesus was a magician and instrument of the devil and that he worked his miracles by the power of the "ineffable name" (Shem Hamphoras). Using cabalistic numerology, the Jews changed Jesus' name into an insult and perverted the conventional Jewish greeting into a curse on Christians. They called Jesus a whore's son and Mary a whore, although they knew better. They claimed that Mary had conceived while menstruating, which meant that her offspring, Jesus, was insane or a demon's child, and they perverted Mary's name into the word for manure pile. Luther recounted, without unequivocally accepting as true, some of the crudest charges traditionally lodged against the Jews: that they poisoned wells, and that they kidnapped children, pierced them with nails, and hacked them into pieces. He believed them guilty in thought and deed of shedding the blood of the Messiah and his Christians.

The Jews' claim that they were held captive by the Christians was a "thick, fat lie." They were free to leave Germany; their departure would be a blessing, for their presence was a plague on Germany. They had been expelled, Luther pointed out, from numerous countries and cities:

France, Spain, Bohemia, Regensburg, Magdeburg, and other places. It was in fact the Christians who were held captive to the Jews' usury.

From this list of indictments Luther swung immediately into the series of harsh recommendations quoted by the Nazi bishop, Martin Sasse. I trust I need not repeat them here. In the closing section of the treatise, Luther ridiculed the Jews' hope for a Messiah who would give them a worldly kingdom but not redeem them from death. He would prefer to be a sow, who had no terror of death, he said, than to have such a Messiah.

Although it might be tempting to do so, we may not dismiss the older Luther's attacks on the Jews as simply the product of an ill and depressed old man who had departed from the tolerant position of his earlier years. Nor may we conclude, as Bishop Sasse did, that experience had transformed a friend of the Jews into a great opponent. There is ample evidence that undermines any attempt to drive a wedge between the younger and the older Luther. [9]

For one thing, Wilhelm Maurer, among others, has convincingly shown that Luther's basic theological view of the Jews underwent little, if any, change from the Psalms lectures of 1513-1515 to the last sermon of 1546. [10] Undergirding all Luther's pronouncements on the Jews, Maurer argues, were four basic theological principles or presuppositions that remained constant through Luther's career. These principles or presuppositions derived from Luther's theology of justification by faith alone with its distinction between law and gospel, judgment and faith. The principles were (1) that the Jews were a people suffering under the wrath of God; (2) that without divine intervention they were incorrigible and impossible to convert by human effort; (3) that their religion remained perpetually hostile to Christianity and could not cease blaspheming God and Christ; and (4) that there existed a "solidarity of guilt" between Christians and Jews: a common suffering under God's wrath, a common resistance to Christ, a common attempt to gain one's own righteousness and salvation apart from Christ, a common need for grace. Except for point 4, asserting a solidarity of guilt, these principles are characteristic of the position held traditionally by Christian theologians. In Luther's case, you can find these principles in the Psalms lectures with which he began his professorial career as well as in the anti-Jewish treatises of his last years. It would appear, therefore, that Luther's *theological* view of the Jews remained constant while only the practical recommendations for their treatment changed.

Not only was the theology constant, but also the harshness was no new element in his work and thought. His polemics were angry and abusive from the beginning. By his own admission, he was an angry man. Anger was his special sin. [11] But anger could also be necessary and proper—and useful. [12] It helped him, he said, to write well, to pray, and to preach. "Anger refreshes all my blood, sharpens my mind, and drives away temptations," he once commented. [13]

But Luther's anger and his abuse of opponents could also spark criticism, and did so from the very beginning of the reformation. For example, in August 1520 Luther acknowledged that "nearly everyone condemns my mordancy." [14] And in his famous appearance before the Diet of Worms in 1521 he admitted that in some of his writings he had been sharper than befitted a monk and professor. [15] In later years he often acknowledged that some were offended by his harshness and anger. [16] But he had an explanation: "I was born to war with fanatics and devils," he wrote in 1529. "Thus my books are very stormy and bellicose. I must root out the stumps and trunks, hew away the thorns and briar, fill in the puddles. I am the coarse woodsman, who must pioneer and hew a path." [17]

This explanation is self-serving, of course, but there is also much truth in it. Luther was a pioneer who used his angry pen to blaze a way and open a path for others. A man of equal theological genius but of another temperament might have broken with the Roman Catholic church and defended the reformed church with less violence and name-calling. It should be pointed out, however, that Luther's colleague, Philip Melanchthon, a man of similar temperament, although not as profound a theologian, believed that the times had required a man of Luther's harshness. [18] In any case, Luther's polemical skills from the beginning played a vital role in mobilizing support for his Reformation insights and program.

A reading of Luther's polemical corpus does leave the

distinct impression, however, that in his later years his anger became more shrill, and less leavened by compassion, humor, or even theological reflection. Moreover, his always pungent language became more coarse and scatological. The targets of his ire become under his pen the vilest of hypocrites, totally wicked and insincere, willing minions of the devil, deserving of the most horrible fate.

The trend toward greater harshness was extended over a number of years. I have shown elsewhere that while the ill health and frequent depressions of the later years undoubtedly exacerbated this characteristic of Luther's personality, these personal changes cannot be said to account for the polemical excesses of the later years. [19]

Even the old Luther was never consistently violent or vulgar in his polemics. Throughout his last years he produced both vituperative and temperate polemics. Consider his attacks on Duke Heinrich of Braunschweig-Wolfenbuttel. In 1541 he produced *Against Hanswurst*, a politically inspired treatise and one of the coarsest Luther ever wrote. Four years later he wrote the moderate *To the Elector of Saxony and the Landgrave of Hesse Concerning the Captured Heinrich of Braunschweig* (1545). [20] The differences between these two treatises can best be explained not by changes in Luther's physical or mental health but by changes in external circumstances. The abuse and coarseness found in the earlier treatise was a deliberate polemical tactic, and perfectly in keeping with the general sordidness of the larger dispute. In the later treatise Luther sought to dissuade the landgrave from releasing Duke Heinrich who had recently been taken prisoner. This called for a calm, reasoned argument, which Luther produced. Furthermore, every polemic Luther wrote during these later years contained sections devoted to clear and persuasive exposition of doctrine and exegesis of Scripture. Once again, his *Against Hanswurst* is illustrative. Fully two-thirds of the treatise is given over to savage, uninhibited (and often unedifying) attacks on Duke Heinrich and his Catholic allies. Yet, sandwiched between the invective and abuse is a lucid discussion of the characteristics of the true and false church and a briefer comment on the distinction between person and office. The independent worth of this section on the true and false church was attested to by its later publication in combination with the "Schmalkaldic Articles."[21] It would appear, as this example illustrates, that the vulgarity and violence was by choice. Luther could turn it on and off as it suited his purposes. His illnesses may have made him more irritable and less inhibited, but he had not lost complete control.

It should also be pointed out that within the context of Luther's polemics, his attacks on the Jews are in no way unusual. Luther did not have a special animus against the Jews; he indulged in even greater vitriol in attacking Catholics. Surpassing his anti-Jewish treatises for coarseness and stridency, for example, is the already mentioned *Against Hanswurst*. Luther outdid even the virulence of *Against Hanswurst* in his 1545 *Against the Papacy at Rome, Founded by the Devil*. On the heels of these treatises he published a series of scatological and violent woodcuts that, in most graphic terms, suggested how good Christians should treat the papacy. In these and other treatises Luther bestialized his opponents, most frequently likening them to pigs or asses, or called them liars, murderers, and hypocrites. He considered them all minions of the devil. He directed the devil to his ass, he renamed the papal decretals "decraptals" /*Drecketalen*/, the Farnese pope "Fart-ass" /*fartz Esel*/ and "Her Sodomitical Hellishness Paula III." He threw around words for excrement with great abandon. And in the woodcuts by Lucas Cranach commissioned by Luther near the end of his life, he had the papal church depicted as being expelled from the anus of an enormous she-devil, had peasants shown defecating in the papal crown, and suggested, once again in picture, that the pope, cardinals, and bishops should be hung from gallows with their tongues nailed alongside.

His attacks on other Protestants and on Turks were slightly more restrained than his attacks on Catholics, but no less severe than his attacks on the Jews.

The explanation for this non-discriminatory vitriol must be sought in his apocalyptic and Augustinian vision of the contemporary world.

Early in his career as a reformer, his reading of the Bible had convinced him that practically from the beginning of the world there had been a perpetual, unchanging struggle between the true and false church.[22] He saw this struggle

as involving a recurrent contest between true and false
prophets and apostles. Believing that mankind did not change
and that the devil never slept, he could trace this struggle
from the biblical histories into his own time. What happened
to the prophets and apostles in their day could and would
happen to the church of his day. Their experiences established
an archetype of the dynamics of all sacred history.

When Luther surveyed his own times in light of this
archetype, he classified the papacy as the antichrist described
in Scripture, the Turks as Gog and the little horn in the Book
Daniel, contemporary Jewry as the remnant of a rejected
people suffering under God's wrath, and his Protestant opponents as contemporary false prophets and apostles, like
those who had plagued the true prophets and apostles.[23] They
were all members of the false church. In fact, all of humanity was divided into these two camps, so Luther understood
his disagreements with all of his opponents in terms of a
cosmic struggle between God and Satan. When he attacked
the Jews or the Catholics or the Turks or the "fanatics," he
was not merely attacking human beings. Rather he was
attacking Satan himself, who, as the spirit behind the false
church, was motivating these opponents. And the issues
separating the true from the false church were not trivial:
they distinguished the saved from the damned.

Luther saw evidence of the struggle between the true
and false church throughout history, but this struggle was
reaching its climax in his own day. Once the Reformation
exposed the papacy as the antichrist seated within the church,
the final battle was joined. Satan unleashed all his minions
in a last, desperate attempt to defeat the servants of Christ.
The world was in the throes of the climactic battle before
the Last Judgment.

Personal disappointment and fears strengthened Luther's
conviction that he was living on the eve of the Last Judgment. Although he had never entertained much hope for the
mass of a sinful humanity, events from the mid-1520s onward
still shocked and disappointed him. He was made particularly indignant by what he saw as widespread indifference
and ingratitude toward the renewed Gospel. This ingratitude,
conjoined often with what seemed to him to be open blasphemy, was interpreted as further signs of the imminence
of the last Judgment.

Luther's apocalyptic mood may also have been reinforced by his fears for the Reformation movement after his own death. These fears were shared by others. Elector Johann Friedrich commissioned the "Schmalkaldic Articles" partly to serve as Luther's "last testament" both against Catholics and against deviants within the Protestant ranks. [24] Luther himself viewed as his last testament against these different opponents his anti-Jewish treatises of 1543, his *Short Confession on the Supper* of 1544, and his 1545 *Against the Papacy at Rome, Founded by the Devil* along with the associated cartoons.

Given his Augustinian dualism and his conviction that the contest was in its climactic stages, it is hardly surprising that his attacks were so severe. Had he not attacked his opponents, including the Jews, with all the vehemence at his command, he would have been like a soldier who shirked his duty in the final, most critical days of the war. When he encountered criticism of the severity of his attacks, he replied that his critics did not realize the enormity of the stakes involved. [25]

His specific recommendations concerning the Jews must also be evaluated within the context of his and general sixteenth-century beliefs about blasphemy and its effects on the community. For Luther a Protestant territory was Christian not because its inhabitants were Christian, but to the extent that it refused to tolerate anti-Christian teaching in public. By the mid-1530s Luther had abandoned his belief that Jewish blasphemy against Christ and God was confined to the privacy of the synagogue. Having encountered Jewish propaganda and received report of active Jewish proselytizing, Luther became convinced that the Jews and their blasphemy were a threat to the public good. His demands—that synagogues be burned and buried, that Jewish prayer books and the Talmud be destroyed, that rabbis be forbidden to teach, and that Jewish worship be forbidden—stem from his belief that Jewish teaching and preaching contained blasphemy.[26] Moreover, he and his contemporaries believed that public blasphemy affected the well-being of the community. Rulers who tolerated blasphemy, whether it was the Catholic Mass, a Sacramentarian view of the Lord's Supper, or Jewish synagogues, violated their

responsibilities as rulers and invited divine punishment for
themselves and their people.

Even so, it must be stressed that the *primary* target of
his anti-Jewish writings was not Jews *per se* but rather Rabbinic exegesis. [27]

Luther placed considerable importance on his Christo-
centric reading of the Hebrew Bible or Old Testament. Luther
believed that the true church of God had been established
even before the Fall when God commanded Adam to eat
from every tree except the tree of the knowlege of good and
evil. When Satan had tempted Adam and Eve, and they
had fallen, God had immediately announced the promise
of the blessed seed that would crush the head of the serpent.
The saints of the Hebrew Bible lived and taught this faith
in the promise of the seed of the woman. "They gave the exact
same sermons that we in our time present to the church and
community of God, except that they taught about the future
Christ who was yet to come, but we say of him: 'Christ has
come,' while they said: 'He will come.' " [28] For this reason
Luther interpreted the Hebrew Bible as referring to Christ.
Following medieval exegesis, he further believed that the
Hebrew Bible testified not only to Christ but to the trinity
as well. [29]

Rabbinic exegesis challenged both views. And under the
influence of humanist scholarship, which placed a premium
on going to the sources and on applying historical and
philological techniques to the sources, Protestant theologians
and exegetes were adopting the more historical and source-
critical opinions of Jewish exegetes.

The bulk of Luther's anti-Jewish treatises consists of an
elaborate attempt to dissuade fellow Protestants from em-
ploying Rabbinic exegesis. He attacked the exegesis itself,
using historical, scriptural, and theological arguments. But
he also employed his rhetorical skills to attack its source:
the Jews themselves. To discredit the message it helps also
to discredit the messenger.

*

What, then, is the contemporary relevance of these historical observations?

1. The anti-Jewish writings must be taken seriously as an accurate expression of Luther's views and as an integral part of his own theological understanding. They cannot be dismissed as aberrations, as medieval remnants, or as the simple products of senility, depression, or ill health.

2. I am a historian, not a theologian or biblical scholar, but I believe I am safe in asserting that three of the central elements in Luther's anti-Jewish writings no longer hold today.

First, few people, I trust, would today share Luther's apocalyptic vision of the struggle between the true and false churches. In saying this, I am not claiming that no serious person sees Satanic forces in the world. The Holocaust has made the reality of evil all too horribly plain. But I do not believe many people today see Satan looming behind all those with whom they have a theological or religious disagreement. And although bellicose remarks emanating from the White House and the Kremlin can generate fears that we could be living in the End Time, it is generally fringe groups within Christianity who expect an imminent Apocalypse. And it is extremists who, believing they are soldiers of the light in the final battle of Armageddon, feel justified in attacking and abusing Jews. Modern anti-Semitism does not normally take this religious form, but rather is fueled by political ideology, nationalism, or racism.

Second, most of Luther's treatises were devoted to defending an exclusively Christological and even a trinitarian reading of the Hebrew Bible. This was a losing cause. Modern Old Testament scholars, I presume, must adhere to the canons of modern historical criticism. Whatever theological interpretations they may make of the Hebrew Bible, they must begin with a historical understanding of the Hebrew Bible much different from Martin Luther's.

Third, the concern that Jewish "blasphemy" would invite divine punishment over the whole community rests on conditions and assumptions that have largely disappeared in the modern world. It presupposes, for example, a single and exclusive state church and a homogeneous religious community that does not exist in today's pluralistic societies.

Moreover, it assumes that God intervenes in human affairs in such a predictable fashion. And, most important of all, it claims a monopoly on religious truth that few would assert so confidently today.

It is, of course, frightening to contemplate that while such exclusive claims and confident convictions are rarely advanced today in the religious realm, it is another matter when we enter the political sphere. There is a secular counterpart to "blasphemy." The twentieth century has seen virulent anti-Semitism and systematic persecution of Jews arise among homogeneous political communities that claim sole and exclusive validity for a particular political ideology. In this regard at least we are no more enlightened than our sixteenth-century forebears.

Having made these observations I must point out that in the strictly religious sphere the root cause of Luther's anti-Jewish opinions remains unresolved, and there seems no way to relativize or historicize this fundamental conviction, for it lies in Christianity itself. Luther makes much of the distinction between Law and Gospel, between those who are slaves to sin and those who are set free by grace. Of course, this distinction is not original with Luther. It is Pauline in inspiration. But its effect, throughout the history of Christian-Jewish relations, has been to consign the Jewish religion to the status of a "has-been." Judaism is seen as a religion of "law" that has now been superseded by a religion of grace revealed through Christ.

I do not know how we might surmount this dichotomy, for it cuts both ways. If one believes that Christ was the true Messiah who established a new covenant between God and Israel, where does this leave those who hold to the original covenant? On the other hand, if one believes that the ancient covenant between God and Israel was not transformed by the man Jesus, where does this leave those who hold to the new covenant? Christianity was born out of, but also in opposition to, Judaism.

Luther, with what for today is certainly unconscionable violence and abusiveness, points nevertheless to this fundamental and all too real opposition. We may overcome the prejudices and hatreds of the sixteenth century, but we still must resolve, or at least learn to peacefully and tolerantly live with, this diagreement.

Notes

1. This talk, in a slightly altered form, was originally given in Stockholm, Sweden, at the meeting of the Lutheran World Federation and the International Jewish Committee on Interreligious Consultations.

2. Much of the material in this essay is taken from my *Luther's Last Battles: Politics and Polemics, 1531-1546* (Ithaca, New York, 1983). See also Johannes Brosseder, *Luthers Stellung zu den Juden im Spiegel seiner Interpreten. Interpretation und Rezeption von Luthers Schriften und Äusserungen zum Judentum im 19. and 20. Jahrhundert vor allem im deutschsprachigen Raum*, (Munich, 1972); Kurt Meier, "Zur Interpretation von Luthers Judenschriften," in *Vierhundertfünfzig Jahre lutherische Reformation, 1517-1967* (Berlin/Göttingen, 1967), pp. 233-252; C. Bernd Sucher, *Luthers Stellung zu den Juden. Eine Interpretation aus germanistischer Sicht* (Nieuwkoop, 1977), pp. 125-199; Wilhelm Maurer, "Die Zeit der Reformation," in *Kirche und Synagoge*, ed. Karl-Heinrich Rengstorf and Siegfried von Kortzfleisch (Stuttgart, 1968), I, 363-452; and Heiko A. Oberman, *Wurzein des Antisemitismus: Christenangst und Judenplage im Zeitalter von Humanismus und Reformation* (Severin und Siedler, 1981); English translation: *The Roots of Anti-Semitism in the Age of Renaissance and Reformation* (Philadelphia, 1983).

3. Of the vast literature on the history of the Jews and of Jewish-Christian relations, I have found most useful Rosemary Radford Reuther, *Faith and Fratricide: The Theological Roots of Anti-Semitism* (New York, 1974); Alan Davies (ed.), *Antisemitism and the Foundations of Christianity* (New York, 1979); Salo Baron, *A Social and Religious History of the Jews* (New York, 1957-1973), vols. II-XV; Guido Kisch, *The Jews in Medieval Germany: A Study of Their Legal and Social Status* (Chicago, 1949); and Jeremy Cohen, *The Friars and the Jews: The Evolution of Medieval Anti-Judaism* (Ithaca, New York, 1982).

4. The critical edition of Luther's works is *D. Martin Luthers Werke Kritische Gesamtausgabe* (Weimar, 1983 —), hereafter abbreviated *WA*. His correspondence is found in *D. Martin Luthers Werke Briefwechsel* (Weimar, 1930 —), hereafter abbreviated as *WABr*. His *That Jesus Christ Was a Born Jew* is in volume XI of the *WA*.

5. WA XI, 336.

6. WA L, 312-337.

7. WA LIII, 439-446.

8. WA LIII, 449.

9. I deal with this issue at some length in my *Luther's Last Battles...*, especially chapter 1.

10. Maurer has published two major essays on Luther's attitude toward the Jews: Wilhelm Maurer, *Kirche und Synagogue. Motive und Formen der Auseinandersetzung der Kirche mit dem Judentum im Laufe der Geschichte. Franz Belitzsch-Vorlesungen 1951* (Stuttgart, 1953); and Maurer, "Die Zeit der Reformation" (see note 2). There are some significant differences between the two essays

(see Brosseder, *Luthers Stellung zu den Juden,* pp. 270-275). In the later essay Maurer places less stress on the missionary aspects of the 1523 treatise and more on its Christological thrust. Brosseder follows Maurer on most points.

11. WABr I, 87 (no. 197).

12. *Ibid.*

13. WABr II, 455 (no. 2410a).

14. WABr II, 168. Luther added, "but I feel as you /Wenceslaus Link/ do that perhaps in this way God is revealing the fictions of men. For I see that which is treated quietly in our age soon passes into oblivion, no one caring about it." Cf. WABr II, 163-164, where Luther also observed, "If every chiding word /*increpatio*/ is a slander /*conuitium*/, then no one is more slanderous /*criminantior*/ than the prophets." For a recent overview of Luther's "cursing," see Martin Brecht, "Der 'Schimpfer' Martin Luther," *Luther* LII (1981), 97-113.

15. WA VII, 834.

16. E.g., WABr VI, 73-75; WA XXX/3, 470; WABr XI, 71.

17. WA XXX/2, 68.

18. *Corpus Reformatorum* XI, 729-730.

19. I offer some statistics for this in my *Luther's Last Battles....* There is considerable literature on Luther's physical and mental health. Among the best is Annemarie Halder, *Das Harnsteinleiden Martin Luthers* (Munich, 1969). See also Friedrich Küchenmeister, *Dr. Martin Luthers Krankengeschichte* (Leipzig, 1881); Wilhelm Ebstein, *D. Martin Luthers Krankheiten und deren Einfluss auf seinen Körperlichen und geistigen Zustand* (Stuttgart, 1908); Erwin Mülhaupt, "Luthers Kampf mit der Krantheit," *Luther, XXIX* (1958), 115-123; and Ethel Bacchus and H. Kenneth Scatliff (eds.), "Martin Luther: A Panel Postmortem," *Chicago Medicine, LXIX* (1966), 107-116. See also, Edwards, *Luther's Last Battles...,* chapter 1.

20. See *Ibid.,* chapter 7, for a detailed discussion of these treatises.

21. WA LI, 466.

22. The literature on these issues is immense. See, among others, Mark U. Edwards Jr., *Luther and the False Brethren* (Stanford, 1975), especially chapter 5; Heinrich Bornkamm, *Luther und das Alte Testament* (Tübingen, 1948); Scott Hendrix, *Ecclesia in Via. Ecclesiological Developments in the Medieval Psalms Exegesis and Dictata Super Psalterium of Martin Luther* (Leiden, 1974); Ernst Schäfer, *Luther als Kirchenhistoriker* (Gütersloh, 1897); John M. Headley, *Luther's View of Church History* (New Haven, 1963); Hans von Campenhausen, "Reformatorisches Selbstbewusstsein und reformatorisches Geschichtsbewusstsein bei Luther, 1517-1522," *Archiv für Reformationsgeschichte,* XXXVII (1940), 128-149; Wolfgang Günter, "Die geschichtstheologischen Voraussetzungen von Luthers Selbstverständnis," in *Von Konstanz nach Trient. Beiträge zur Kirchengeschichte von den Reformkonzilien bis zum Tridentinum. Festgabe für August Franzen,* ed. R. Bäumer (Paderborn, 1972), pp. 379-394; Wolfgang Höhne, *Luthers Anschauungen über die Kontinuität der Kirche* (Berlin/Hamburg, 1963), pp. 124-156; and Ulrich Asendorf, *Eschatologie bei Luther* (Göttingen, 1967), pp. 214-221.

23. The summary in this and the following paragraphs is drawn from my *Luther's Last Battles...* and *Luther and the False Brethren*. The interested reader should consult these two books for a detailed examination of the primary material undergirding this overview.

24. The history of the origin, original purpose, and status of these articles has been the subject of research and controversy. See, among others, H. Virck, "Zu den Beratungen der Protestaten über die Konzilsbulle vom 4. Juni 1536," *Zeitschrift für Kirchengeschichte*, XIII (1892-1893), 487-512; Hans Volz, *Luthers Schmalkaldische Artikel und Melanchthons Tractatus de potestate papae* (Gotha, 1931); Ernst Bizer, "Die Wittenberger Theologen und das Konzil 1537: Ein ungedrucktes Gutachten," *Archiv für Reformationsgeschichte*, XLVII (1956) 77-101; *Idem*, "Zum geschichtlichen Verständnis von Luthers Schmalkaldischen Artikeln," *Zeitschrift für Kirchengeschichte*, LXVII (1955-1956), 61-92; Hans Volz, "Luthers Schmalkaldische Artikel," *Zeitschrift für Kirchengeschichte*, LXVIII (1957), 259-286; Ernst Bizer, "Noch einmal: Die Schmalkaldischen Artikel," *Zeitschrift für Kirchengeschichte*, XVIII (1957), 287-294; and Hans Volz (ed.), *Urkunden und Aktenstücke zur Geschichte von Martin Luthers Schmalkaldischen Artikeln 1536-1574* (Berlin, 1957). On Elector Johann Friedrich's intentions, see Volz, *Urkunden und Aktenstücke...*, pp. 23, 83-91.

25. E.g., WABr XI, 71.

26. See Maurer, "Die Zeit der Reformation," pp. 421-422.

27. *Ibid.*, pp. 416, 407-415.

28. WA XLIV, 635.

29. For a more detailed examination of these views, see, among others, Scott Hendrix, *Ecclesia in Via...*; James Samuel Preus, *From Shadow to Promise: Old Testament Interpretations from Augustine to the Young Luther* (Cambridge, Massachusetts, 1969); Jaroslav Pelikan, *Luther the Expositor* (St. Louis, 1959); and Bornkamm, *Luther and das Alte Testament*.

THE GERMAN PROTESTANT
SOCIAL DILEMMA:
FROM BISMARCK TO HITLER

William O. Shanahan

The German Protestants' relation to the modern world has been closely tied to the vicissitudes of Germany's national history. The terms of the Reformation made their churches dependent on princely governments which produced the coordinated civil-ecclesiastical system known as the *Staatskirchentum*. Dependence on princes, and later the monarchs, nurtured the churches' consistent conservatism. Since the Reformation succeeded, among other reasons, because the princes protected it, German Protestantism became embodied in numerous territorial churches instead of a single church. These churches have successfully resisted every effort to unify them, although revolutionary and political threats have obliged them to accept a collegial or federal relationship with one another.[1]

The Reformation also left Germany divided in its religious loyalties with Lutheranism and Catholicism the predominant confessional forms. Calvinism, or the Reformed faith, attained only a modest presence limited to the Palatinate and some south German enclaves. All the Lutheran churches have been distinguished by their persistent emphasis on doctrine. That emphasis has heightened the importance of theology as well as of the university professors who have been its custodians. The Lutheran ecclesia often seems to consist of theologians, then the clergy and the laity. It also sustains a firm ecclesiastical and liturgical outline. That disposition together with the churches' close governmental ties helps to explain why the sects have not prospered in Germany. Before the middle of the eighteenth century, extra-church movements were not tolerated, and even thereafter they attracted few adherents. Free churches patterned after the established ones have been more successful.

In recent times the varied theological currents and the rise of church parties have loosened doctrinal and liturgical conformity. By acknowledging the church as an ecclesia such variations as Pietism and Free Protestantism became tolerable. Real dissent occurred only on a modest scale, at least before the Third Reich, so that a German "chapel" has never challenged "the church." The outcome has deprived Germany of the kind of support generally provided by sectarians or low-church groups for tolerance and social reform as well as for parliamentary government and democracy. The weakness of Calvinism, both in numbers and political presence, has also tended to diminish the German Protestant anxiety about the bearing that worldly affairs can have on the realization of human aspirations.

That statement does not refer so much to social indifference as to inherent theological constraints. Luther's theology did not make the church a *regnum* analogous to the state; it had authority but it lacked dominion. Authority to rule which came from God belonged to the prince or the magistrates. They had a Christian obligation to rule so as to fulfill God's purpose in the world. They had to be obeyed in all things, not out of fear, but out of religious conviction. Obedience was enjoined because the free exercise of will could only lead to sinfulness. For Luther the universe was not ruled by a uniform, rational law; Creation and all its works bore the taint of sin and evil that had sunk deeply into every Christian. The world contained a terrible *Dämonie*, a power of evil capable of breaking into and disrupting human efforts.

Government, although itself a part of the sinful world, existed to keep sin and evil at bay so as to make possible the work of the church. As set forth by Luther the church lacked well-defined institutional characteristics. It had a spiritual not a formal presence. But it had the responsibility for preaching the Word, the New Testament promise that Christ's sacrifice had revealed God's redeeming grace that enlivens faith and makes redemption possible. God seeks the human heart through the church's preaching of the Word. It alone promises salvation because the human mind by itself cannot know God's intention, nor can it know His cosmic design. This theology did not acknowledge any hierarchic connection between the divine will, the natural order, or even the just laws of the commonwealth. If the positive law was to have just attributes, the prince or the magistrates had to see to it. Their laws fulfilled the justice of the world which was determined solely by right reason and in conformity with worldly necessities.

Every Christian lived, therefore, in two distinct realms. One, inward and spiritual, was characterized by suffering, anxiety, and submissiveness to God's righteousness. The other, the realm of Creation or the natural, secular world, remained wholly subject to civil governance, which maintained order and preserved the justice that was proper to human affairs. To the civil authority belonged all the rules and ordinances that bore on men's occupations, governed their households, and determined their civil obligations. Neither the church nor the civil authority could by itself do God's work in this world. They had to act in concert, to become coordinated so that on the one hand the Gospel did not become civil law, and on the other, that the civil laws did not become preliminary means for gaining salvation. Christians could show the reality of their faith by obeying civil authority and by practising charity and brotherly love in a manner which fulfilled the functions of the household and the *ordo politicus.*

Luther's teaching about the two spheres of rule — God's *Regiment* and that of the sinful world — could be extended in general terms to all the situations experienced by Christians. Its principal outcome was to dramatize the Christian duty to serve the political order as a work of love and obligation even though the civil authority lacked an intrinsic ethical value because it shared in the sinfulness of God's Creation. The separation of secular and spiritual realms meant that the world had its own set of rules, its *Eigengesetzlichkeit.* Worldly rules partook of the evil in the world so that tyranny and injustice remained a mystery to believing Christians.

That outlook had far-reaching political implications. The misuse of power could not be sinful since power came from a sinful world. What was sinful was the temptation for individuals to revolt against or to resist that power. This contrasts with the classical and humanistic formulation that the misuse of power is immoral, or even criminal.

In Germany, the modern state, with Prussia setting the prime example, took up the charge that Luther had laid on civil authority. It sustained the princely absolutism that found its most complete expression in the rule of the post-Reformation *Landesvater*, the pious princes who strove to fulfill their Christian obligation to their subjects. By the nineteenth century Prussian usage set the tone for the German Protestant understanding of politics and statecraft. Hegel, Stahl, and Ranke, each in his own way, strengthened the Lutheran-Protestant *Staatsethos*. It gained credibility because most Prussian rulers did cling to their sense of moral rulership exercised in responsibility to God.

TOWARD A SOCIAL GOSPEL

Luther's theology reflected a deeper concern for sin than for human suffering. But the temper of the modern world has gradually made human suffering one of its principal concerns. The onset of industrialism gave rise to a need for a Christian response to the plight of working people caught up in the new economic system. Among the German Protestants the recovery, early in the nineteenth century, of foreign missionary zeal and efforts to spread the Gospel among heathen people, provided a vehicle for a Christian mission to the urban, industrial poor.

Johann Hinrich Wichern (1808-1881) launched this effort near Hamburg in the 1830s. He called it the Inner Mission, an agency for charitable ministering to German Christians living in material want or in despair. Wichern's tireless efforts, his organizing talent, and the urgency of the Revolution of 1848 gave the Inner Mission the momentum and the importance that enabled it to become a national institution. It embraced all phases of remedial and charitable activities in a national organization that worked within all the territorial churches with its own charities and welfare activities that complemented the existing ones.

Wichern appeared to accept the Lutheran teaching about the polarity of church and state so that, as a churchman,

he only strove to overcome "spiritual pauperism." Even that
goal presented theological difficulties because it seemed to
make the Inner Mission a surrogate for the church. Equally
suspect at that time were Wichern's ideas about the "holi-
ness of the nation."

Wichern's deep antipathy to the liberal political goals
sought in 1848 combined with his strong support for the
Prussian government in the revolutionary crisis to enable
him to find a public footing in the reactionary fifties.
Wichern's own conservatism left no doubt about the legitimacy of monarchical institutions, the existing class structure,
and private property. Only the abnormalities and distortions of an idealized agrarian-monarchical world disturbed
him. He did acknowledge that the social distress brought
about by urban impoverishment had created a "disconnected
estate," a social category lacking conviction about traditional values and therefore open to radical persuasion. Urban life and factory employment seemed to him to be the
environments which nurtured an anti-Christian outlook.
His attitude left a legacy of anti-urbanism that subsequently
burdened Evangelical-Protestant social efforts. But lack of
social insight was not Wichern's only problem. His efforts
to create an Evangelical-Protestant social mission suffered
because he stirred up confessional opposition by his attempt
to make all the faithful a universal priesthood, to transform
the increasingly sacramental state churches into a *Volkskirche*. His ideal of a *Volkskirche* eventually became a key
element in the German Protestants' sense of their identity
with the German nation.

Wichern's celebration of the national unity achieved in
1871 gave it Christian attributes that heralded the subsequent Protestant-Christian apotheosis of the German Empire.
He endowed the new Fatherland with a spiritual function
as a sanctuary in which Christians had a better chance of
attaining heaven. He proved willing to depart from contemporary confessional orthodoxy without sacrificing its strong
attachment to a romantic-conservative distaste for an urban-
industrial society. Wichern's theological non-conformity
lacked a social counterpart. As a consequence he had little
insight into the reality of increasingly complex social issues.
His efforts did not promote social reform so much as they

did a theological debate about the respective roles of church and state in a modern society. He made charity the basis of Christian good works, and the vast Inner Mission organization testified to the German Protestants' readiness to match his Christian zeal. But his legacy also included a sense of the union between Protestant faith and the German nation.

PROBLEMS OF A CHRISTIAN SOCIAL ETHIC

Wichern's deeply conservative political outlook reflected the revolutionary experience in 1848 that had driven the Evangelical-Protestant churches into a closer protective relationship with traditional monarchical governments. It confirmed all the Christian churches in their resistance to any profound social or political change because it appeared to be morally disruptive and to promote irreligion. Under Pius IX (1846-1878) the Roman Catholic Church condemned the political and intellectual currents stirred up by modernity. The German Protestant churches, fortified by the counter-revolutionary success and an accompanying revival of a stern theological orthodoxy, also set their face against the modern age. Schleiermacher's theological opening to an embrace of modern culture remained an unused passage for almost a century.

The Evangelical-Protestant vision of the world presumed a stable set of God-ordained institutions: a patriarchal household and an echelon of social ranks corresponding to occupations and civil functions, all embraced within a legitimate and, customarily, a monarchical political authority. All the exceptional social elements had easily recognized characteristics: the halt and the lame, the aged, widows and orphans, alcoholics, criminals, and so forth. Charity took care of their needs, solely in a remedial, not corrective, sense. Thus the initial Evangelical-Protestant response to industrial ills stressed an intensified personal obligation to care for the sick and needy. German Pietism helped to authorize and to expand that effort.

Wichern as well as other contemporaries with strong Evangelical-Protestant social convictions, such as Victor Aimé Huber (1800-1869) and Hermann Wagener, grasped the industrial working class' mood of despair and uncer-

tainty. They agreed that the nation faced a serious threat
of social dissolution, but all their suggested countermeasures
rested on a personal response based on an ethic of Christian
charitable responsibility. They did not understand the profound structural change in society that accompanied the
growth of towns and industry. Their conservative vision still
obscured what other observers had begun to call "the social
question," the critical relation of a new social category, the
fourth estate, to the traditional social order. At first only
the religious imperative alarmed Evangelical-Protestants
because the spread of industry and the growth of towns sustained a steady process of dechristianization. The customary
countermeasures appeared to be sufficient: forming new
parishes, building more churches, and intensifying the
Diakonie, that is, the whole range of charitable efforts.

A great deal of well-intentioned charitable effort went
into the practical work of assisting and sustaining unfortunate persons suffering illness or poverty. A modest start in
a more practical direction took shape in proposals for a cooperative movement. Wickern had endorsed it but it remained
for Victor Aimé Huber to attempt to organize a consumers'
cooperative and a cooperative savings bank. Neither proved
successful and their failure doomed Huber's intention of
providing factory workers with such amenities as detached
houses with running water, gas, baths, and small gardens.
Huber remained convinced that better material circumstances, especially good housing, would raise the level of
working class moral and family life. But he failed to convince Wichern and the Inner Mission that saving the working class from moral decay required a constructive economic
program, not merely charity.

Improved administration of charity took precedence
over other means of assistance. In textile manufacturing
cities of modest size (ca. 100,000 inhabitants), such as
Elberfeld and Barmen, a predominant Protestant population with marked pietist inclinations created an excellent
system of publicly administered poor relief. The Elberfeld
system which came into being in 1853 recognized the insuf-
ficiency of voluntary charitable activity because it did not
acknowledge that poverty, identified as a lowered standard
of living, had multiple causes and one in particular, un-

employment. The Elberfeld system, which could be considered to be a Protestant achievement, enjoyed a practical success that inspired its adoption by many German cities.

The national acclaim enjoyed by the Elberfeld poor relief methods undoubtedly marked the German Protestants' increasing readiness to engage the public authorities, either the urban or the regional governments, in an expanded poor relief as well as regulatory legislation. It implied a clearer perception of the range and depth of personal distress that accompanied the growth of an urban-industrial society. But that perception still lacked a definition of the churches' social responsibility other than an intensified and more efficiently administered charity.

The German Protestants did not succeed in forming a realistic social ethic before the 1880s. This delay cannot be explained solely in theological terms. A meaningful social ethic requires an understanding of society as a reality sufficient to itself. That understanding was lacking in Germany until well into the nineteenth century. And the initial attempts to theorize about modern society made by Tönnies and his successors drew on the general categories provided by German Idealism rather than empirical studies. These were singularly lacking in Germany. Max Weber's study of East Elbian agricultural labor made in the early nineties was the first large-scale empirical account to come to public attention. German literature also failed to overcome this deficit of social information. It lacked "social novels" that portrayed and explored the depths of the human situation. Realistic literature finally burst on an astonished German public in the nineties with Gerhart Hauptmann's play, *The Weavers* (1892) and Paul Göhre's autobiographical account, *Three Months in a Factory*. Of course the German public's lack of social knowledge was not exceptional. Jacob Riis's investigative reporting on the plight of the American urban poor revealed previously unnoticed conditions. And, for the British public, Mayhew's deft reporting on London's poor became more explicit in Booth's surveys made from the 1880s on.

Forming a modern Christian social ethic also requires an objective study of social institutions in a manner that places the church as an institution among all the others. Evangelical-Protestants proved reluctant to do that since it implied an abandonment of such key Lutheran concepts as the "two realms of being," and the fulfillment of both social and moral obligations in individual "callings" or occupations.

To cope with the nineteenth-century social question Germany was favored by the persistence, even in an age of laissez faire, of traditional governmental responsibility for the general welfare. It had originated in the patriarchal guidance of the *Landesvater* and it became more sophisticated in the regulatory efforts of the enlightened rulers. What was called *Polizei*, or the full administrative range of public welfare measures, including police, schools, public health and morals, agricultural and technical improvements, and so forth, provided the basis for an Evangelical-Protestant response to the social question. A specific content for this effort, both for the government and for an emerging Evangelical-Protestant social ethic, came from the challenge to market economics made by prominent German academic economists. These "socialists of the chair," as their opponents called them, favored state intervention to deal with social needs. Their ranks included such eminent figures as Gustav Schmoller and Adolf Wagner, the latter a devout Christian who entered wholeheartedly into the evangelical-social movement.

THE SOCIALIST CHALLENGE

The immediate cause of an Evangelical-Protestant social initiative came from the startling vigor shown by the newly organized Social Democratic party. Its leaders had taken a stand against the Franco-Prussian War. But despite their disdain for patriotic sentiment, in the Reichstag elections of 1877 the Social Democrats received one vote in seven for a total of a half million. This impressive success by an avowed Marxist party which openly proclaimed its hostility for both religion and the existing social order aroused general alarm. But the origin of evangelical social action in response to the Social Democratic challenge set up a lasting tension between Protestant social sensibility and socialism. The Social Democrats' anti-religious propaganda appeared to give socialism a daemonic character, something beyond assimilation or control that could only be exorcised.

Evangelical-Protestants already stirred by the Protestant zeal displayed by the government in the *Kulturkampf* could readily support Bismarck's effort to suppress socialism. That it entailed a break with his uncomfortable parliamentary alliance with the liberals made the new direction of his program even more acceptable. It began with the socialists' suppression in 1878 followed in 1881 by Kaiser William I's formal announcement of impending social legislation. Between 1883 and 1889 it brought Germany a comprehensive social insurance program which Bismarck repeatedly justified as a form of "practical Christianity."

Whether Bismarck did act as a Christian statesman, or whether he sought pragmatically to show the industrial workers that they had something to gain by remaining loyal subjects, has long been a moot point. Bismarck, it should be noted, was not a formal member of any church and his religious observances took very personal, pietistic forms. Notwithstanding, Bismarck's social insurance program sanctioned by a devout Protestant monarch had the attributes of an Evangelical-Protestant response to an urgent social-political issue.

It had that appearance because, as Hans Rothfels has observed, Bismarck acted in the Lutheran spirit by relying on the state's own civil justice to counteract a social distortion. And Bismarck understood himself to be a deeply religious servitor of a monarch who fulfilled God's purpose in the world. As a Lutheran Christian, Bismarck understood the dualism of power and conscience, between purpose and means in political affairs. He had complete confidence in the state, in the Prussian monarchical state, not nationalism nor democracy. He did not believe in progress or the goodness of mankind. He set himself against all the contrary forces within and without Prussia that threatened the solidarity of the throne. He ruled out political compromise and strove to crush every domestic adversary. Against foreign dangers he let his own conscience be the measure of the appropriate response, taking care that a resort to military force would not be unlimited. He was thoroughly committed to a Lutheran *Staatsethos.*

Unfortunately Bismarck exaggerated the strength and durability of the domestic institutions that he sought ruthlessly to preserve. In the long run, as his successors discovered, his methods failed to stabilize either domestic or foreign affairs.

By accepting a Lutheran definition of his political responsibility Bismarck set the terms of subsequent Evangelical-Protestant efforts to deal with social issues. German Protestants enthusiastically approved his social insurance program as a fully qualified evangelical-social reform. They put their seal of approval on its political format. They endorsed the correlation between a Christian motive in social politics and a governmental response because it upheld the civil authority's obligation to respect and fulfill the religious requirements of earthly life. Responsible civil measures brought a certain closure of the realm of grace and the realm of creation. Until 1918 the system of state churches, which linked church and state through the monarch's authority as the *summus episcopus*, seemed to provide that mutuality of civil-religious effort. The outcome made for a pronounced political basis for Evangelical-Protestant concern for social reform.

Along with Bismarck, the evangelical-social movement became identified with the social reform effort of other state officials. A very prominent one was Theodor Lohmann (1831-1905), a Prussian civil servant who had provided Bismarck with the actuarial and financial data pertinent to the Sickness Insurance Law (1883). Lohmann subsequently assisted Freiherr von Berlepsch (1843-1926), the Prussian Minister of Commerce, during William II's short-lived enthusiasm for expanding Bismarck's social law-giving (1890-1896). Even Graf Posadowsky, Reichs-Minister of the Interior (1897-1907), also gained evangelical-social honors for having authorized minor extensions of the existing social legislation. Conversely, the state's monopolistic social intervention meant that supplementary measures such as charitable relief, hospices, and settlement houses came to have a predominantly religious character.

STOECKER'S POPULIST APPEAL

All the theological and political proprieties were violated by Adolf Stoecker's (1835-1909) personal response to the socialist challenge. This military chaplain, who had shown an intense patriotism in the aftermath of the Franco-Prussian War, had been rewarded with a post as a Prussian court chaplain. In 1878, dismayed by what he judged to be a socialist revolutionary surge in Berlin, he launched, in the name of Christian responsibility, his own Christian-Social party. In defiance of both church custom and court etiquette he took to the hustings himself to deliver fiery blasts at the Social Democrats. Despite grievous personal faults, including his persistent anti-Semitism, Stoecker proved to be a dynamic evangelical-social leader. He left a legacy of social-political activism that came to maturity in the Weimar period.

Stoecker was a product of Pietism who became absorbed in the national pathos of the Bismarck era, a mixture of piety, religious confidence, and national pride. But as a man of humble origins he understood the injustice of the urban workers' plight. He proposed to remedy it by making the church sponsor reform legislation based on the "Socialism of the Chair."

Stoecker spent his life caught between his sympathy for the oppressed and his ambition to gain ecclesiastical and political prominence. He also strove to live in an opulent *bürgerlich* style. One image made him a protagonist of the working class who fought to raise its aspirations and secure its rights in both church and state. Another and more personal image disclosed Stoecker to be a social climber who cultivated the rich and powerful. As director of the Berlin *Stadtmission* he had entree to the social world of his patrons, the court, the nobility, and wealthy burghers. For many of his contemporaries Stoecker's vanity, his ambition to become "rich and famous," made his social convictions seem insincere.

Nonetheless, they were genuine. He understood that the industrial workers made up a loyal and legitimate element in the German nation, an association pointedly denied by Bismarck. But Stoecker's sympathy did not arouse an electoral response. His Christian-Social party enjoyed little success in his initial attempt to get the Berlin workers' vote. When his direct electoral bid failed he shifted his attack to political liberalism and its economic doctrine, Manchesterism. To give that attack an emotional intensity he introduced

anti-Semitism to German parliamentary politics, a dubious
gambit that has tarnished Stoecker's historical reputation.
Political anti-Semitism soon escaped his grasp to take on
sordid racial overtones. Still, Stoecker persisted with his
Christian-Social vision and, working within the Conservative party, he eventually succeeded in placing an anti-Semitic
plank in that party's Tivoli Program of 1892.

Stoecker's career suffered because he challenged the
massive state envelope around evangelical-social efforts.
As an ordained minister he violated clerical protocol by taking
Christian perceptions about social issues into electoral politics. Nor could he disguise his rivalry with Bismarck, who
had immediately perceived Stoecker's political party as a
threatening evangelical analogue to the Catholic Center
party. Even the enactment of social insurance legislation did
not bring Stoecker any relief because Bismarck, with characteristic paranoia, persisted in identifying him as a personal
rival. Prussian church officials did not spare him either.

Ecclesiastical guidelines for the Prussian Protestant clergy's
concern for social issues zigzagged back and forth with the
government's shifting social policy. Screened by the Socialist
Law, the *Oberkirchenrat*, the Prussian United Church's
governing body, directly admonished Stoecker. It lifted its
cloture rule slightly in 1881 to endorse the imperial message,
and it opened it wider in 1890 when the young Kaiser William
II, suddenly enamored of social reform, announced that
he wished to become "King of the Beggars." He soon lost
interest and yielded to the conservative persuasion of the Saar
industrialist, Baron Stumm. Another church directive then
brought the clergy back into line with the government's new
outlook favoring repressive measures.

NEW REFORM CURRENTS

A new generation of evangelical-social activists came to the
fore among the Evangelical-Protestant clergy in the 1880s.
They were partly inspired by Stoecker's zeal, although many
eventually rejected his anti-Semitism. More continuity among
them developed from the inspiration provided by Albrecht
Ritschl (1822-1889), the outstanding systematic theologian
of the Bismarck era. His system shared the readiness of

Protestant theology to absorb contemporary intellectual and political conventions except that Ritschl's theology enabled theological scholarship to combine with liberal-historical convictions. Ritschl helped to inspire what came to be called *Kulturprotestantismus*, a heady mixture of personal religious convictions, optimism about the promise of modern culture for mankind's liberation, as well as confidence that the modern national state provided the proper vehicle for making this transformation possible.

The *Ritschlianer* came from every theological school, attracted by Ritschl's return to the "historical Jesus," whose ethical teachings were said to be the core of New Testament revelation. Ritschl had absolute confidence that historical scholarship would confirm his interpretation. Ritschl also introduced a strong existential emphasis which enabled him to banish metaphysics, mysticism and philosophical speculation from his theology. It did, however, bear a strong neo-Kantian imprint. Ritschl envisaged God as a "loving Father," not as a judge. According to Ritschl faith manifested itself in ethical actions, in moral fulfillment of love of others in a Kantian sense. For Ritschl an outgoing, morally expressive faith would begin to realize a moral and cultural realm in this world in anticipation of the *Reich Gottes*. By moving theology away from dogmatics toward ethics Ritschl went a long way toward overcoming the *aporia* of formal Lutheran social thought. His teaching offered a theological basis for a comprehensive reordering of Evangelical-Protestant assumptions about Christian social responsibility.

Ritschlian views sustained the formation within the older liberal theological school of a more progressive group known as the Free Protestants. Ironically, its leading members, Martin Rade and his associates who founded the weekly, *Christliche Welt*, in 1887; Friedrich Naumann (1860-1919), who won fame as a political publicist; and Adolf von Harnack, the founder of historical theology, all came from rigorously Lutheran families and had attended the most stern confessional Lutheran universities. Their breach with the past became manifest in 1888 when Harnack's father, a strict Lutheran professor of dogmatics at Dorpat, joined the opposition against his son's appointment to the University of Berlin. Eventually Kaiser William II intervened to assure Harnack's

tenured professorship. From that prestigious post Harnack
played a key role in spreading Ritschlian views as well as
propagating a new sense of Protestant responsibility for dealing with the ills of an urban-industrial world.

FOUNDING THE EVANGELICAL-SOCIAL CONGRESS

Bismarck's dismissal in 1890, the end of the Socialist Law,
and Kaiser William II's "New Course," which promised
additional social legislation, stirred all the social-reform-
oriented Protestant groups. It brought together a broad
coalition that ranged from Stoecker's coterie on the right to
the Free Protestants on the left. It included government
officials and prominent academicians, among the latter Max
Weber, Hans Delbrück, Adolf Wagner, and Rudolf Sohm.
A shift in the Inner Mission's previous aloofness from social
and economic issues opened the way for orthodox Evangelical-
Protestants to participate. Lohmann's widely circulated study
of the tasks of the church and the Inner Mission in respect
to the urgent social and economic issues of the day had much
to do with the change of heart among the orthodox faithful.
Naumann, who had been engaged as a young pastor in Inner Mission work, lent his considerable journalistic talent
to publicizing the argument presented in Lohmann's *Die
Aufgaben der Kirche und ihrer Inneren Mission gegenüber
den wirtschaftlichen und gesellschaftlichen Kämpfen der
Gegenwart* (1884).

On Stoecker's initiative this coalition formed the Evangelical-Social Congress in 1890. It proposed, as a Christian
assembly standing apart from the church, to study the nation's
social and economic problems, to judge them by religious
requirements, and to make recommendations for both leg-
islative and charitable relief. Through an annual meeting,
press coverage, and publications, the Congress hoped to
awaken the Protestant social conscience and to sustain the
government's intention of augmenting its existing social
political program.

Although the Congress professed both a theological and
a political neutrality, neither current politics nor theological
differences could be kept at bay. Some social issues invariably
bore strong political overtones. They surged through Weber's

account of East Elbian agricultural labor in 1894 which offended conservatives and contributed to the breakup of the Congress. Theological rivalries also broke into the open. A Free Protestant faction gathered around Naumann had become disenchanted with Stoecker, especially his anti-Semitism. Stoecker, for his part, could not abide their modern theological, anti-conservative outlook. The lapse in the Kaiser's social reform interest also seemed to doom the Congress' public mission, especially when it became known that the Kaiser (in a telegram to his former tutor, Hinzpeter, on February 28, 1896) had said that "Christian-Social is nonsense."

Stoecker would not compromise his belief that the Congress should seek to re-enforce the church as a commanding ethical force in public life. He conceived the church as an autonomous moral agency capable of acting with the state to assure the moral and social health of society. His vision of an independent church's moral agency included a large measure of social responsibility. But such concepts were too bold for most of his orthodox contemporaries. His own followers in the Christian-Social party did remain faithful to his ideal of church independence. It flowered in the aftermath of Germany's defeat in World War I in the guise of a *Volkskirche* that would undertake to rebuild the nation and restore it to moral and political vigor.

A different set of ideas had begun to prevail in the Evangelical-Social Congress by the mid-nineties. Liberal theologians and Free Protestants looked to the state and to the values of modern culture to provide moral and social sustenance. Stoecker and other orthodox members of the Congress became increasingly dissatisfied. Finally, in 1897, they felt obliged to leave the Congress and form their own assembly, the *Freie kirchlich-soziale Konferenz.*

Two rival conceptions of religion's role in the modern world now confronted one another. The *Konferenz's* program specifically denounced the Evangelical-Social Congress's attempt to exploit human suffering for the futile purpose of achieving the *Reich Gottes.* That statement affirmed the *Konferenz's* theological orthodoxy as well as a conventional church affiliation which enabled it to become a valuable technical auxiliary of the Inner Mission. Unlike the Congress which sought only to shape public opinion favorable to social reform, the *Konferenz* undertook practical engagements. Under Pastor Ludwig Weber, one of Stoecker's most trusted lieutenants, the *Konferenz* promoted the Evangelical Workers' Associations and stood by their participation in the (Catholic) Christian Trade Union movement. Weber steadfastly backed this collaboration despite the German Catholic hierarchy's and the pope's vacillations about the propriety of an inter-confessional labor movement. Papal approval in 1912 eventually made possible a significant Protestant-Catholic cooperation in promoting Christian trade unionism. On the eve of the war almost a quarter of its membership came from some 172,000 Protestant industrial workers enrolled in the Evangelical Workers' Associations.

THE FREE PROTESTANT DISENGAGEMENT

The Evangelical-Social Congress had provided a forum for Friedrich Naumann to display his extraordinary range of talent. The Congress's crisis had also coincided with a crisis in Naumann's conception of his public mission. Its religious imperatives had become much weaker. By the early nineties he had become disenchanted with the prospect that he could stir the Inner Mission into more vigorous social reform activity. In turn, the Evangelical-Social Congress had not been able to sustain his hope that a Protestant social reform movement could penetrate the working class and elevate it to full religious and political dignity. He persisted in that hope even though his personal efforts to rally working-class groups had not been successful. He had perceived the Social Democrats' moral validity and he had shocked churchgoers, as well as his ecclesiastical superiors, by referring to them as a "modern Christian heresy."

That statement also reflected the mounting tension between Naumann and the church authorities over his doctrinal soundness and questionable political loyalties. His drift into secular life accelerated in the mid-nineties when he was drawn into the nationalistic excitement being generated by public discussion of imperialism, naval armaments, and *Weltpolitik*. His mounting social imperialist views gained credibility when his friends, Weber and Delbrück, con-

vinced him that neither a religious nor a humane social effort that was held within domestic parameters could cope
with the nation's social issues. Rudolf Sohm, the great
authority on Roman and canon law, also proved very persuasive by arguing that Christ's kingdom was not of this world.
In 1895 he bluntly advised the Congress of the Inner Mission
to avoid combining Christian good works with social concerns under the guise of a Christian-social effort. Sohm
told Naumann even more bluntly: there cannot be a visible
church and the state is a heathen. [2]

His friends' persuasion re-enforced Naumann's readiness
to embrace a career in journalism and politics that made
an end to his close involvement with the evangelical-social
movement. Thereafter he retained only a peripheral interest
in it, except for the Evangelical-Social Congress, because
it had fallen under the control of liberal theologians and
Free Protestants. In 1896 when Naumann launched his own
political party, the National-Social Association, he became
a professional politician. Shortly thereafter he left the ministry. His political party—which was not an antecedent of
National Socialism—made the first of several unsuccessful
attempts to achieve a broad mobilization of liberals and
progressives as well as the less doctrinaire Social Democrats.
For lack of electoral success his party collapsed in 1903 forcing
Naumann to seek his political fortune with the Progressives.

Naumann's odyssey from the church to politics involved
more than a personal journey: it stood for the receptivity of
the well-educated Protestants, the *Bildungsbürgertum*, for
the state idolatry of integral nationalism. By 1898 with
Admiral Tirpitz's first massive naval increase, Naumann
had become an enthusiast of battleships as key instruments
of national power. Only through power, Naumann argued,
could Germany carry out a successful *Weltpolitik*, for national survival depended on gaining colonies and overseas
markets. A bold imperialism coupled with social reform
could bring prosperity and national integration so that the
Reich could become a plebiscitary caesarism under Kaiser
William II. Power political methods received Naumann's
full endorsement because they belonged to the inner logic
and rules, the *Eigengesetzlichkeit*, of foreign affairs. National
states had complete freedom to identify their own ends

as well as the means for achieving them. Here Naumann
betrayed the Lutheran principle that civil authority must
always live up to its Christian responsibility. He had
succumbed to the *Dämonie* of power.

Naumann's embrace of politics deprived the evangelical-
social movement of his extraordinary talents. He was an
accomplished speaker who also commanded a lucid prose
style. His magnetic personality attracted and held his many
and varied friendships. He pursued his objectives with tireless energy. He lived selflessly to serve the nation as he had
once served his parish. But his intense nationalism typified
the hubris of the Wilhelmians. His abandonment of the
ministry together with his immersion in modern culture
made his religious commitment seem to be loose and fragile.

Most churchgoers made the same judgment about the
Free Protestants, especially those associated with the peri-
odical *Christliche Welt*, all of whom were prominent advocates of evangelical-social action. Its editor, Martin Rade,
a superb journalist with a flair for organizing and taking
part in publicity-oriented conferences, had a wide range
of interests. But his evangelical-social advocacy was com-
promised by his eclectic range which included too many
daring positions. Rade flirted with pacifism; together with
many Free Protestants he entered unashamedly into international religious congresses that mixed Christians with
non-Christians; he also shared an ecumenical hope for the
Christian world. The Free Protestants, as a liberal group,
also reacted to every tremor in church affairs so that the
editorial resources of their journal were invariably deployed
to defend clerics brought up on charges of doctrinal or liturgical inconsistency. Such daring comprehensiveness made
it difficult for the *Christliche Welt* circle to persuade orthodox believers to become social witnesses.

Christliche Welt generally held aloof from political
controversy, although the *Daily Telegraph* affair in 1908,
which displayed the Kaiser's naiveté about the conduct of
foreign affairs, drew some sharp editorial comment. But
no positive steps were taken in its aftermath to bolster the
attempt to form a political coalition of left liberals and right-
wing Social Democrats, the so-called front "From Bebel to
Bassermann."

Liberal theologians and the *Christliche Welt* circle had been forced to pay more attention to church politics because church officials had begun to take strong disciplinary measures to preserve orthodoxy and guard against modernist intrusions. Their action bore a resemblance to the Catholic Church's struggle to overcome the Modernist crisis which had matured at the beginning of the twentieth century. In both the Catholic and the German Protestant worlds social concern languished in the face of bitter doctrinal strife. But unlike the Catholic modernists the German liberal modernizers had more defensive resources.

In 1904 the German theological liberals established an annual forum, "The Friends of *Christliche Welt*." Its organizing principles made clear its intention of forming a defensive block opposed to the over-zealous measures being used by church authorities to control theological opinion and to shape uniform pastoral methods. This organization did not diminish Rade and his associates' vigorous advocacy of social reform through the Evangelical-Social Congress, chaired after 1912 by the liberal theologian, Otto Baumgarten. It continued to feature leading German academicians whose proposals and comments provided an expert view of social politics. Whether they influenced social opinion within the various territorial churches is doubtful. Each religious group seemed to be talking to itself because the nation had begun to subordinate religion to its secular concerns.

RELIGIOUS VERSUS POLITICAL CULTURE

By the early 1900s the Protestant imperatives of national life had declined in importance. A lethargy had settled over the German Protestant community and its remaining energies seemed to be spent in disciplining refractory clergymen for doctrinal and liturgical irregularities, or wasted in internal quarrels of the kind that had split the Evangelical-Social Congress. By 1902 even the *Christliche Welt* circle of Free Protestants, ordinarily a tolerant and accommodating group, got into a squabble with the older liberal theological organization, the *Protestantenverein*. Ecclesiastical Protestantism had indeed been pushed to the edge of na-

tional affairs because it had not kept pace with the national
political mobilization which had started in the nineties.

That mobilization had brought about a deepening of
political culture with a corresponding increase in political
awareness, including more readiness to turn critical issues
into political channels. The active electorate expanded with
more voters turning out for elections. A "political Germany",
more secular than religious had come of age thanks to general literacy, an active press, and the introduction of popular propaganda and electoral techniques. [3] Very modern
methods, including the use of film, characterized the opinion-
making efforts of various special interest groups, some associated with political parties and others independent. They
included the Colonial Society, the Navy League, the Pan-
Germans, and the H-K-T Society which fought against the
Polonization of East Elbia.

Political parties also adopted the vigorous new methods,
even the Conservatives whose Farmers' League captured a
radical agrarian revolt in southwest Germany. Other parties
responded by forming ongoing local organizations and by
relying more on party professionals with full-time staffs.
The Social Democrats, released from political limbo in 1890,
set about building a powerful bureaucratic party machine
and intensifying their effort to form a working class subculture. Large-scale trade unions and *Mittelstand* organizations also came into the picture. An unsigned but continu-
ously observed alliance between the Social Democratic party
and the Free Unions created a new and powerful force in
German parliamentary affairs.

German Catholics did not lag in their efforts to participate in the national political mobilization. To the Center
party's well-established footing in the Catholic parishes came
the support of the Christian Trade Unions (1894 ff.), while
the *Volksverein* with a half-million members orchestrated
the cause of the party, the Christian unions, and Catholic
social action.

The Protestant effort fell short because it was undoubtedly
engulfed by the effective mobilization of opinion for political, economic, imperialist, or naval armament causes. As
a Protestant auxiliary the Evangelical-Social Congress had
started brilliantly, but its promise of reaching a national

audience could not be fulfilled. Similar organizations such as the *Kirchlich-Soziale Konferenz* or the *Freunde der Christlichen Welt* attracted limited and mutually exclusive audiences. Other national Protestant organizations showed the same aloofness from one another, the most notorious being the *Christliche Welt* group's disdain for the Inner Mission. Although the annual Inner Mission congresses had begun to discuss social topics, that agency remained powerless to expand either its functions or its appeal. Other national organizations such as the *Gustav Adolf Werk* and the *Protestantenverein* appeared moribund. Only the *Evangelischer Bund* showed any degree of vigor and that went into its unrelenting struggle against Catholicism. It kept the spirit of the *Kulturkampf* alive by emphasizing the mystical bond between Protestantism and the German Reich. Its success undoubtedly measured the Protestants' gradual acceptance of a nationalist ideology.

THE PROTESTANT EMBRACE OF NATIONALISM

Devout Protestants had not embraced nationalism at the time of German unification. Their loyalties remained dynastic and regional in keeping with the German particularist political tradition. To these Protestants the nationalist ideology was badly tainted by its association with the liberal movement in both politics and theology. Theological liberalism, the counterpart of political liberalism, had strong commitments to national church unity and to the assimilation of Protestantism in modern culture. To orthodox churchgoing Protestants political liberalism stood for unbridled egotism and complete endorsement of all the rational and scientific aspects of modern culture as well as efforts to separate church and state. Both liberal parties did present a wholly secular countenance. The National Liberal program of 1867 did not mention the church nor religion, while that of the Progressives, in proposing civil equality for all religious beliefs and associations, advocated the separation of church and state. [4]

At midcentury many Protestants, especially those in the north and east, clung to an idealized conception of the Prussian monarchy which would be endangered by its merger into a national state. The Evangelical-Protestant churches had greeted the outbreak of war in 1866 and 1870 with a summons to prayer and penance. As Bismarck directed the sequence of events that did bring national unity, several confessional theologians, Martin Kähler among them, cautioned against the "idolatry of the state." Protestant fears about the suppression of the territorial churches in the regions annexed by Prussia — Schleswig-Holstein, Hanover, and Hesse — were not immediately set at rest despite Bismarck's caution in addressing that issue.

Those fears rose in October, 1871 when the achievement of national unity prompted liberal elements to discuss national church unity as its corollary. At this *Oktoberversammlung* Wichern spoke up for the merger of all the territorial churches in the Prussian United Church. Nothing came of his proposal because it could not be promoted in the face of the *Kulturkampf's* threat to the civil prerogatives of both the Catholic and Protestant churches. Despite Protestant uneasiness about the German national state, its realization did have a certain religious resonance. The Prussian soldiers had fought valiantly under the slogan, "Mit Gott für König und Vaterland." As the Prussian War Minister von Roon observed, it appeared to be God's will that allowed Prussian arms to prevail.

Some evangelical doubt clouded the state's struggle with Catholicism in the *Kulturkampf.* But such a stern Biblical pietist as Martin Kähler could insist that the Christian's highest duty was obedience given to a state which he believed to embody selfless service and incorruptibility. The *Kulturkampf* undoubtedly intensified the Protestant identity of the newly created Reich even though its constitution lacked a formal ecclesiastical connection. Protestants gradually began to accept a Christian-conservative *Reichspatriotismus* that gloried in the solid *bürgerlich* values that had helped to create the new nation. The non-Prussian Protestant churches respected the conservative character of the Reich and began to honor it as well as their own dynastic allegiance. By the end of the seventies the ebbing of the *Kulturkampf,* the failure of the church unity movement, and Bismarck's break with his liberal parliamentary supporters set the stage for the gradual conversion of the Evangelical-Protestant faith-

ful to German nationalism. Early in the eighties student
movements picked up the burgeoning nationalistic theme
to extol the triad, "Deutschtum, Kaisertum, Christentum."

Any lingering Protestant fears about the political threat
to autonomous ecclesiastical governments were set aside
when the middle and orthodox church parties gained control of the synods—elective church parliaments—set forth
in the new church constitutions adopted in Prussia and in
other territorial churches. In these relaxed circumstances
the Evangelical-Protestants could join enthusiastically in
the national celebration of Luther's fourth centenary in
1883. This *Lutherfeier*, supported by almost all the territorial churches, and patronized by various princely families
including the Hohenzollerns, made up the first genuine,
deeply felt Protestant celebration of German national unity.

The celebration began the process of turning Luther
into a national hero. Previously he had been perceived only
as the father of the most strict Lutheran confessional
churches.[5] Another national Protestant hero also came
to the fore. By the eighties the veneration that attached to
Friedrich von Bodelschwingh (1831-1910) attained the level
of a national cult. He was a heroic, saintly figure engaged
in missionary activity, hospitals for incurable victims (Bethel,
1873) and worker settlements (Wilhelmsdorf, 1882). As an
indefatigable seeker of alms, Bodelschwingh carried his
charitable plea into every corner of the land. His tireless efforts evoked deep pride among Evangelical-Protestants and
his charities seemed to prove that the united German nation
had deep spiritual roots. To protect them, a nationwide
organization, the *Evangelischer Bund*, came into being in
1886. It promoted the Protestants' Germanic identity in an
aggressive campaign to contrast Catholic universalism with
the Protestants' national loyalty and patriotism.

Hubris is an ingredient of every nationalism and the
German Protestants had reason to be proud of the Reich:
it enjoyed an unparalleled political success. Bismarck had
become Europe's foremost statesman; German city-planning
and urban administration excited international admiration;
foreigners flocked to German universities; and the Prussian
army inspired imitation far and wide, even to the general
adoption of the *Pickelhaube*, the spiked helmet.

The Evangelical-Protestant national perceptions deepened
with the transformation of the Reich into a functional central government. By the eighties this process was well underway. As a consequence the dynastic rulers of the *Länder*
lost ground to the Hohenzollerns. The princes themselves
hastened this process because the post-1871 generation of
regional rulers lacked the political vigor of their fathers.
William II benefited from this shift of dynastic allegiance
because by the 1890s public attention had moved away from
the other German crowned heads to concentrate on him.
He was bold, or tactless, enough to emphasize the change
by condescending to his fellow princes as lesser rulers. The
strengthening of Evangelical-Protestant loyalty to the Kaiser
had much to do with their acceptance of nationalism as a
necessary corollary of the Reich's monarchical government. [6]

The receptivity of German Protestantism to the changing
terms of political guardianship had enabled nationalism to
envelop the Lutheran realm of civil authority. Political
Eigengesetzlichkeit — the moral autonomy of politics — made
the assertion of national power appear to be a necessity of
successful rule. Since contemporary political wisdom interpreted international rivalries as an ongoing struggle for national survival, the fate of the German Protestant people
seemed to depend on the German Empire's forceful diplo-
macy and military strength. And with the deepening of the
Volk's mystical attributes the German nation gradually became one of God's *Ordnungen* in the Evangelical-Protestant image of the world. The full theological development
of this conception of the nation — *das Volk* — as a divinely
ordained institution awaited the outbreak of World War I.

WAR AND REVOLUTION

World War I removed the last vestiges of restraint from
the expression of Evangelical-Protestant national loyalties.
Throughout the first year of the war the clergy unanimously
supported the German cause. After 1915 doubts arose among
the Free Protestants about the wisdom of prolonging the
conflict and especially about the exaggerated annexationist
war aims. On the strict confessional side the clergy redoubled
its patriotic efforts to sanctify German military successes as

God's manifest endorsement of the German mission. Their exaggerated patriotism created what has been called a *Kriegstheologie* characterized by the deliberate merger of Bethlehem and Potsdam. The clergy's wartime sermons also began to contrast the Lutheran basis of German national life and culture with the Calvinistic basis of the democratic western nations. This distinction survived the war to become an historicist ingredient of popular nationalism as well as a profound historical issue to be assessed by German academic learning. [7]

In 1917 the territorial churches and their clergy gave clamorous support from the pulpit and in the church press to Hindenburg and Ludendorff's patriotic front called the Fatherland party. In contrast, only a few scattered Protestant pastors had rallied to endorse the Reichstag's 1917 peace resolution. Any wartime suggestions about parliamentary or electoral reform invariably aroused the Protestant clergy's ire. About 500 clergymen petitioned the Kaiser not to endorse a change in the Prussian electoral law. And not surprisingly the Protestant clergy made a sharp protest against the constitutional reforms proposed late in 1918 by the Chancellor, Prince Max of Baden. Even before the end of the war the Evangelical-Protestant clergy had set themselves resolutely against democracy on the ground that it violated their *protestantischen Staatsgesinnung*. According to this view democracy would challenge Christian life and perpetuate the immorality that, from the clergy's standpoint, had seized the German people in wartime. More basically, it expressed the Protestant clergy's fear about the security of the existing ecclesiastical system if it were to come under the scrutiny and control of popularly-elected representative bodies. These attitudes did little to prepare the Evangelical-Protestant clergy for either Germany's military defeat or for its democratic aftermath.

The sudden collapse of the German war effort and with it the overthrow of all the princely governments in Germany came as a staggering blow to the German Protestant community. Until the eve of the Armistice the church leaders and pastors had persisted in their conviction that God would lead the Germans to victory. A military defeat was wholly unexpected. The republican revolution which followed appeared to place the churches at the mercy of the "God-less Social Democrats." Historians have sometimes complained that the German Revolution was not thorough enough. Nonetheless, most German Protestants experienced it as a caesura which cut them off from their traditions: close ties between throne and altar; the sanctity of monarchical rule; and the overthrow of what had been a mighty pillar: "The Holy Protestant Empire of the German Nation."

Only the Free Protestants and some scattered religious socialists were prepared to acknowledge the legitimacy of the new republican government. For the others it was tainted with the multiple sins of *Gottesleugnerei*, or atheism; democratic arrogance about making worldly improvements; and rebellion against God-ordained authority. Well into 1919 the territorial churches continued to offer prayers for the departed noble rulers. The postwar pattern of hostility to the republic and a longing for a monarchical restoration had set in.

The critical political situation required German Protestants to become active in supporting political parties pledged to uphold their interests. Believing Protestants rallied to the new German National Peoples' party which sought to embrace all the traditional and conservative elements in German life. At the outset the party spoke only of parliamentary government, not the republic, an evasion that subsequently became more explicit when the party aired its monarchist sympathies. Members of Stoecker's Christian-Social party took a very active part in launching it. Many church superintendents and clergymen joined the party; the chairman of the Prussian United Church's general synod sat on the party's directing committee.

Another party with Christian and veiled monarchical sympathies came into being through Gustav Stresemann's efforts as the German Peoples' party. As a successor to the National Liberals it seemed uncertain about church and state relations, a quandary that made it less attractive to clergymen and committed Protestants. Throughout the Weimar period the believing Protestants suspected that liberalism harbored strong secular and anti-clerical designs. That attitude tended to consolidate the electoral support of the faithful and most church leaders for the German National Peoples' party. It cooperated closely with church officials, and until 1928 (when it became the party of Big Business) it served church interests in both the Reichstag and in the regional parliaments.

On the theological left the Free Protestants and some of the old guard church liberals rallied to the new Democratic party, which endorsed the republic as well as the separation of church and state. Those positions condemned it in the eyes of faithful Protestants, who were also repelled by its leadership which included Rade, Naumann, and Troeltsch. Each had, in a strict Protestant view, betrayed either the nation or its church. Rade's fault consisted of his support for the wartime peace movement and a war aims policy of no annexations. Naumann had become persona non grata to church leaders as a secular humanist and religious dilettante. And despite Ernst Troeltsch's (1865-1923) zealous personal war effort, he stood condemned for his readiness to replace religion with a value system based on modern culture. Churchgoers were also repelled by Martin Rade and the *Christliche Welt*'s support for a "people's church" that would bring democracy into ecclesiastical government. The sympathy for socialism expressed by Rade and Baumgarten proved equally offensive to the body of believing Protestants. For these reasons the hope that the Democratic party with its Free Protestant constituency could gain other Protestant adherents and awaken an understanding and sympathy for democratic republican government proved illusory.

The political parties that conservative Protestants were depending on did poorly in the elections to the National Assembly held in 1919. The German National People's party and the German People's party got barely fifteen percent of the votes. The outcome intensified Protestant fear that the Social Democrats would now proceed to dismantle the church, a fear made plausible by the harsh restrictive measures being proposed by the newly-appointed Prussian Minister of Education, the doctrinaire Independent Social Democratic politician, Adolf Hoffmann. But his anti-religious fanaticism aroused such a combined Protestant and Catholic protest that he was forced out of office early in 1919. Nonetheless, the experience confirmed many Protestants in their conviction that the republic posed a danger to religion, the church and the clergy.

The initial decisions of the National Assembly proved to be more favorable to the churches than the Protestants had dared to expect. Thanks to Naumann's leadership and support from a very large contingent of church-oriented members (274), the National Assembly approved constitutional articles very favorable to the churches. They gained stature as public corporations with control of their own properties, as well as a claim on tax support and the right of self-government. The settlement preserved the territorial church system without seriously impairing ecclesiastical autonomy. But the churches' self-government was qualified by the continuance of the state's legal supervision. The legacy of the *Staats-kirchentum* persisted even under republican government.

POSTWAR ADJUSTMENT

What postwar adjustment meant in practice became clear in the ensuing struggle over restructuring the churches that went on within the *Länder*. The Weimar constitution's guidelines had to be implemented by the regional government's enabling legislation. In Prussia and in Saxony the Evangelical-Protestant churches immediately encountered arbitrary governmental intervention in their internal affairs. In Prussia the Social Democrats pursued their own *Kulturkampf* with a vengeance. When Communist governments briefly held power in Thuringia and Saxony the church and clergy fell victim to serious mistreatment that included threats of bodily harm and murder.

The unstable and hostile political environment together with the ruinous inflation of the immediate postwar years left the churches and clergy in dire straits. The central government seemed powerless to restore political and economic stability. Some part of the church members' initial contempt for republican government stemmed from the harsh experience of the early postwar years. Evangelical-Protestants were also chagrined that the Roman Catholic Church seemed able to make satisfactory progress in its negotiations with the *Länder* governments. The conclusion of concordats prompted the evangelical church leadership to follow the same route. The territorial churches in Baden and in Bavaria did succeed in negotiating concordats in 1924. A similar solution in Prussia languished because the *Landtag* did not endorse the Old Prussian Church's new constitution until 1926. After more tedious negotiations a Prussian concordat, adopted only because of massive Social Democratic abstentions, became law in 1931.

These tribulations contrasted with what appeared to be the Catholic Church's success in coping with the new republican government. It enjoyed a national parliamentary presence in the form of the Center party which also manifested enough flexibility to get along with regional governments under Social Democratic control. The Protestants' chagrin was not eased by the acknowledgment that the Center party's parliamentary support had made possible the favorable settlement accorded the churches in the Weimar Republic's constitution. For most devout Evangelical-Protestants, an unpatriotic atmosphere clouded German Catholicism. In wartime such Catholic political leaders as Matthias Erzberger (1875-1921) had made themselves unpopular with the most zealous Protestant patriots. Nor had they forgotten the papal efforts to bring about a negotiated peace. Continued tension between German Protestants and their Catholic compatriots ruled out any collaboration in dealing with either the Communist or the radical nationalist threat to the Weimar Republic. Undoubtedly the continued Protestant resentment of Catholics' prominence in the Weimar Republic contributed to their readiness to embrace the "movement for national reconstruction" that eventually entered into the political appeal of the National Socialists.

The immediate postwar plight of both Protestant and Catholic churches would have been eased by a centrist-conservative Christian political party. But neither the Catholic Center party nor the evangelical church leadership considered it seriously. Between 1918-1920 only two efforts were made in that direction. One initiative came from Adam Stegerwald, leader of the Christian Trade Unions; the other came from young Catholic intellectuals such as Heinrich Brauns and his associates in the Catholic *Volksverein*. The latter group sought a broadbased Christian party that would

be free of the Catholic hierarchy's influence and would be
more positive about democracy and the Weimar Republic.
Stegerwald proposed to stress the natural ties between Catholic
conservatives and Protestant nationalists. Only a handful
of Protestant pastors in Berlin hearkened to this plea. It
failed to stir the Catholic electorate which was not ready to
desert the Center party. And most Evangelical-Protestants
still endorsed the anti-Catholic message of the *Evangelischer
Bund*.

The Evangelical-Protestant social concerns which had
seemed to be maturing around the turn of the century suffered from doctrinal conflicts and the obsessive nationalistic fervor shown during the war. In the postwar period
the institutional survival of the churches became the para-
mount issue so that evangelical-social action languished. Once
that survival had been assured, the Evangelical-Protestant
concern in the public forum focused on enacting a national school law. Neither the Weimar constitution nor the courts
provided adequate guarantees that the clergy could continue to control confessional instruction. Catholic-Protestant
rivalries also clouded the issue inasmuch as Protestants resented having to accept parity with Catholics in a religiously
neutral state. In both Prussia and Saxony what might be
called "a school civil war" broke out. Even Pastor Reinhard
Mumm, who had been an ardent Christian-Social advocate,
referred to the school question as the focus of the churches'
struggle against secularization. By 1928 the shifting party
balance in the Reichstag ruled out any chance of passing
national educational legislation. But the school question
had enjoyed a notable success in mobilizing both the Evangelical-Protestant clergy and large numbers of the laity to
deal with a public concern of the Protestant religious community.

RELIGIOUS SOCIALISM

In the postwar period the German Protestant social advocacy fell largely to the religious socialists. Before the war
only isolated individuals such as the Swiss pastors, Hermann
Kutter (1869-1931) and Leonhard Ragaz (1868-1945), and
the Swabian pastors, Johann Christoph Blumhardt (1805-

1880) and his son Christoph (1842-1919), had advocated religious socialism. They acknowledged the massive Social Democratic party as God's warning as well as an epiphany of a reign of virtue. The religious socialist movement gained vitality and adherents in 1918/1919 when Christians had to confront the possibility that socialism might become a viable economic alternative. Around Marburg a Protestant group known as the *Schlüchtern Kreis* accepted Swiss leadership that included, in 1918, Karl Barth, who still adhered at that time to the Ragaz school. A larger group which first assembled in Baden spread out over south Germany to advocate a *Volkskirche* which would be a closely knit, religious-social community. Another group, eventually the most influential, gathered in Berlin under the aegis of Paul Tillich, Emil Fuchs, and Georg Wünsch. They published the *Blätter für religiösen Sozialismus* in which Tillich began to expound his theology of *kairos*, the fulfillment of time, the "right time," when the eternal element present in the secular socialist movement would break into the secular world and transform it.

In the early postwar years the religious socialist cause gained a modest strength because its aims coincided with the left theological and the south German pietistical view about the necessity of organizing a *Volkskirche*. In this understanding the *Volkskirche* would not presume to be the visible oracle of the nation; it stood only for a greater degree of congregational autonomy as well as an acceptance of a broader range of theological convictions. Above all, this conception of the *Volkskirche* stood for the complete independence of the church, its freedom from the Weimar Republic's insistence on its right to continue to supervise ecclesiastical affairs, to continue, in effect, the *Staatskirchentum* of the past. Support for a *Volkskirche* providing autonomy for the church as well as individual congregations was strongest in Baden, Württemberg and in Rhenish Prussia. But the link between these aspirations and the religious socialists proved to be tenuous because the prospect of a congregational *Volkskirche* soon became remote. As the old territorial ecclesiastical governments recovered their bearings and with it their confidence, they vigorously asserted their ecclesiastical governance of all the faithful. At the same

time the religious socialists went off in a radical direction
that proved distasteful to the congregationalist and liberal
Protestants.

Among the Berlin religious socialists a sympathy for
Marxist historical interpretation became evident because
they undertook the first serious dialogue between Marxism
and Christianity. The Berlin group strove without success
to engage Protestantism with the socialist movement, both
Social Democratic and Communist. All the religious socialists, but particularly those in south Germany, hoped to reconcile socialism with the Church by infusing it with the
superior moral values of liberal Protestantism. Religious
socialists also shared a conviction held generally throughout
the German Protestant community that national cohesion
could be re-enforced by strengthening religious belief. Only
the Berlin group neglected the church in favor of the pro-
letariat. But the Berlin religious socialists' efforts to gain
respectful attention from the socialist parties drew the same
rude scorn that Lenin had shown for Ragaz in their sole wartime encounter in Zurich. And despite the religious socialists' intellectual vigor, which enabled them to transcend their
doctrine's Swiss origins, religious socialism failed to stir the
mass of the German Protestants; it lost ground by the mid-
twenties and became the concern mainly of a small intellectual enclave. Faithful churchgoers held fast to the Lutheran
rejection of humanistic interventions in this world as well as
to the futility of efforts to banish sin and corruption from it.

THE CONSERVATIVE THEOLOGICAL RENEWAL

Evangelical-social concern suffered after 1918 from the
collapse of *Kulturprotestantismus*. From about 1900 it had
been one of the principal custodians of that concern as sym-
bolized by Harnack's honorary chairmanship of the Evangelical-Social Congress (1902-1912). But Germany's military
defeat and the deep sense of cultural crisis felt by many intellectuals doomed the optimistic, progressive outlook favored
by liberal theologians and the Free Protestants. And by
1919-1920 religious orthodoxy regained its intellectual com-
posure from Karl Barth's commentaries on the *Römerbrief*,
St. Paul's *Epistle to the Romans*. This publication ter-

minated Barth's religious socialist ties and announced the format of his Dialectical Theology, or theology of crisis. It rejected even more decisively than Lutheran doctrine all the previous programs and methods for achieving a Christian social effect.

Because Barth declared God to be "wholly other" such efforts were not only futile, but illegitimate. To the German Protestant clergy, bewildered by the disintegration of their world, Barth sounded like an Old Testament prophet calling for a religious rebirth. Despite Barth's Reformed antecedents they hearkened to his radical demand for a return to preaching the Word. Their social concerns went into decline. Tillich has commented on the difficulty throughout the twenties of arousing theological candidates' interest in social issues.

Evangelical-social activity persisted despite this unfavorable atmosphere. It survived in the provincial by-ways of Protestant life, especially among the Westphalian and Swabian Pietists, the "quiet in the land," who had previously been skeptical of political parties. They became more politically-minded because they perceived the irresponsibility of the extreme nationalist right as well as the impossibility of winning the German National Peoples' party's support for social reform. Some Christian-social advocates such as Pastor Reinhard Mumm remained in that party but many others left it to support the Weimar coalition parties, the Social Democrats, and the Center. Both elements kept their social focus on the *Kirchlich-Soziale Bund* (successor to the *Kirchlich-Soziale Konferenz*) and its programs, most notably the sponsorship of the Evangelical Workingmen's Associations and the specialized training of Protestant labor secretaries.

These efforts found their theological and ethical warranty in the teaching of Friedrich Brunstäd (1883-1944), who promulgated an ethic of social political responsibility derived from an idealist unity of culture, the nation and the state. In German Idealism he found the means for regaining cultural values and overcoming the contemporary crisis. Brunstäd had no blueprint for a Christian society; instead he proposed a struggle for a righteous social order based on God's ordinances for the structure of temporal affairs. The correct example had been set, in his judgment, by Wilhelmian

Germany. But Brunstäd's backward glance did not lack real insight: he defended temporal authority in a genuine Lutheran spirit that enabled him to recognize the aberrations of the nationalist right as well as the absurdity of the Nazi's racial doctrines.

Those Evangelical-Protestants who kept the promise of Christian social action alive held aloof from the resurgence of conservative Lutheran theology. Postwar bitterness and disillusionment conspired to turn many theologians toward a vigorous renewal of conservative Lutheranism. The darkened times and Barth's challenge aroused the confessional Lutherans, who sensed their opportunity in the liberal theologians' discomfiture and in the widely shared sense of a deep cultural crisis. Their theological renewal concentrated on Luther, who had already been woven into the fabric of German nationalism. An intensely emotional celebration occurred in 1917, a critical year of the war and the fourth centenary of Luther's Ninety-five Theses. That celebration had also included Karl Holl's severely scholarly address on Luther's understanding of religion. He dealt entirely with young Luther's struggle to find his way to God, a theme that exercised a strong postwar appeal to Evangelical-Protestants. Holl's scholarship inspired a "Luther Renaissance" which quickly flowed into a political theology intent on justifying a neo-conservatism that identified Evangelical-Lutheranism with the German nation, with its monarchical authoritarianism and its irrational depths. The New Lutheran theology stimulated a flood of popular and quasi-learned writing which spread disillusionment and doubt about democracy as well as almost every other aspect of modern culture.

The New Lutheranism broke down the Evangelical-Protestant theologians' traditional restraint about drawing broad social and political conclusions directly from Christian teaching. [8] They exploited the conservative doctrine, first systematically studied during the Restoration, of God's *Schöpfungsordnungen*, or the divinely ordained social categories. The traditional ones had been the church, the state, the family, and the various occupations. The ethical norm of each *Ordnung* tended to be taken wholly from the prevailing usage so as to sustain conformity and diminish challenges to God's prescribed arrangements. In their fully developed theological form the *Schöpfungsordnungen* stood guard against sin although they formed part of the sinful world. Because they originated both in Revelation and in historical experience, new ones could be added. Friedrich Brunstäd held that the *Ordnungen* included the whole capitalist economy. Much more significance attached to the theologians' readiness to consider the German people and their nationality, the nation itself, as part of God's creation. Their affirmation of the German nation's divinely ordained status could be used to justify an augmented state authority which had an obligation to defend and preserve the nation's cultural and ethnic identity.

Most dialectical theologians condemned the extended teaching about the *Schöpfungsordnungen* as a serious error. Nonetheless, it had a very broad appeal, evident in its use by Hirsch, Elert, Althaus, Brunstäd, Wünsch (a religious socialist), Gogarten, Brunner (dialectical theologians), and Erich Foerster (a Reformed pastor associated with *Christliche Welt*). Not every theologian carried the doctrine to extreme lengths. Yet it did make possible a vulgar synthesis of German nationalism and Christianity which divinized the nation so as to condemn whatever seemed harmful to it — the Versailles Treaty, internationalism, pacifism, parliamentary government, and even the ecumenical movement which had begun to flourish in the postwar period. The Weimar Republic could be denounced for its inability to protect the German nation's basic right. From this assumption, Paul Althaus (1888-1966) developed a moral possibility unique in post-Reformation Lutheranism, the right of resistance to a government which had failed to preserve the nation as the norm of the state's existence. There were other consequences.

The conservative theological position which became dominant after World War I derived much of its assurance from Germany's military defeat. Unchastened by that defeat the conservative theologians developed a view that the war had been a great moral test imposed by God on the nation, a test which the nation had failed. Defeat had come about because of moral weakness and the breakdown of national solidarity. Conservative theologians were not alone in that belief. In the Weimar period a profound sense of a need for a revived and vital national community became one of the most widely shared assumptions about Germany's recovery. That sense had arisen and had been strengthened by the war experience, especially by what its most sincere and convinced advocates called the *Fronterlebnis*, the "front experience." Subsequently, the republican and radical features of the 1918-1919 revolution, particularly its leadership by political parties and social elements that seemed, to conservatives, to be alien to the German community, fortified the deep yearning for a restoration of national communal vitality.

The German Protestant churches which had been ardent advocates of Germany's war effort had no difficulty in accepting a theological explanation of military defeat that also upheld their essential role in rebuilding the nation as a solid communal block. In that urgent task the church claimed equal stature with the state. That claim rested on a conservative theological understanding of the *Volkskirche* which differed sharply from the congregationalist-latitudinarian definition. The conservative theologians interpreted it in terms appropriate to the Reformation: the *Volkskirche* was an all-embracing ecclesia, that is, a formal body that embraced the whole population, the believers as well as the unbelievers. By preaching the Word the church offered the nation the promise of God's grace that would enable it to recover its moral and communal foundations. The church leaders' pervasive belief in their obligation to be the guardians of German culture, a conviction intensified by the Protestants' warm embrace of German nationalism, added intensity to the church leaders' eagerness to meet and fulfill their national responsibility.

By defining the nation as one of God's natural institutions the conservative theologians strengthened their claim to preside over its moral recovery. In reality the circumstances of postwar Germany, and the marginal role of the territorial churches, made their claim an exaggeration of religion's public stature. In practical terms their claim focused attention on the churches' demand for clerical supervision of the moral and religious content of primary education. Since the primary level was almost entirely a governmental activity, the conservative assumptions about the essential role of the church in the urgent task of national reconstruction made the form and content of religious instruction one of the most crucial public issues. A prolonged parliamentary struggle over that issue inevitably became a major preoccupation of the Evangelical-Protestant churches and their members. It mobilized the clergy and laity in sufficient strength and with an intensity of feeling that dampened their concern for social issues affecting the industrial working class.

Linking the school question to the religious aspects of national recovery sharpened the Protestants' nationalistic sensibility. A proud nationalism inclined many church leaders and most of the churchgoing laity to recognize allies in various nationalistic movements that resented the humiliation of the peace terms and denied the legitimacy of parliamentary government. It stirred many sincere Protestants to become Christian witnesses to the German nation's recovery of its political strength and vitality.

TOWARD THE THIRD REICH

The Christian witness inevitably took on its own political attributes. Until the presidential elections of 1925 which brought Hindenburg into office, the political outlook accompanying the *Volkskirche* mission had a pronounced monarchical character. Thereafter it settled into an uneasy compromise with the parliamentary system which lasted as long as the German National Peoples' party remained heir to the Wilhelmian tradition of conservatism. For most Evangelical-Protestants the German Empire (1871-1918) provided the standard by which contemporary political circumstances continued to be judged. And as a natural corollary of that view Bismarck took on the stature of an ideal statesman, even one who had acted in terms of deeply felt Christian principles. A cadre of extreme *völkisch*-nationalistic theologians that included Reinhold Seeberg, Emanuel Hirsch, Paul Althaus, and Wilhelm Stapel took this historical leitmotif a step further to proclaim that German history partook of God's revelation. History had defined the divine purpose of the German national mission. None of these

theologians openly advocated National Socialism, at least
in its early stages, but their invective rhetoric tended to discredit parliamentary government and to arouse sympathy
for an authoritarian political settlement.

By the late twenties the Protestant laity began to part
company from the church leadership in respect to their political convictions. If the leaders lacked a warm affection
for the Weimar Republic they did acknowledge that the
several *Länder* governments continued to subsidize clerical
salaries and to permit, in varying degrees, an element of
religious instruction in primary schooling. Political disagreement between the laity and the church leaders remained
masked as long as the German National Peoples' party remained faithful to its German conservative antecedents.
By 1928 the most sincere Evangelical-Protestants began to
lose confidence in that party because it fell under the control
of Alfred Hugenberg (1865-1951), the press lord and cinema
magnate, and his associates from large-scale industry. The
most devout, and the most socially committed Protestants
followed the leaders of what had been the Christian-Social
party in an exodus that searched for another political haven.
Various Protestant splinter groups sought to become political parties; among them only the *Christlich-Sozial Volks-
dienst* achieved any degree of electoral success.

By 1928-1929 the onset of the Great Depression and the
electoral revival of the National Socialist party created difficulties for a specifically Protestant political recovery. Protestant sympathy for radical nationalistic movements and even
for their racial content had already begun to be expressed
publicly. Otto Dibelius and Adolf Schlatter, both able theologians as well as respected church leaders, had defended
a racial definition of Germany's national revival. By 1930
the question of the churches' relation to National Socialism
had given rise to heated discussion in all church circles.
Those who advocated a closer relationship enjoyed a rhetorical advantage by insisting that the churches could not
stand apart from the ground swell of nationalistic fervor
that accompanied Nazism.

That fervor had also been borne into the sphere of
ecclesiastical government, into its elective features in the
parishes and synods. The German Christians who had not

previously been identified with National Socialism now, swollen in numbers, had become its advocates within the body of the Evangelical-Protestant community. Small evanescent cults of "German Christianity" based on Paul de Lagarde, Houston Stewart Chamberlain, and Artur Bonus had appeared in the aftermath of World War I. These cults remained obscure with little influence or impact on Protestant church life. Throughout the twenties the Evangelical-Protestant churches showed little interest or concern about Hitler and the Nazis. Less than two hundred Protestant clergymen, out of a clerical population of about 20,000 ventured to join the National Socialist party before 1930.

Before that date the Nazis were very careful to preserve their appearance of being neutral with respect to religion. Hitler discouraged those party enthusiasts who wished to carry the National Socialist message into the councils of the territorial churches. He strove to present a respectable image of bourgeois nationalism, even disparaging some of the ruffians who fought the party's battles in the streets. But after the party's great electoral success in 1930 the National Socialists became bolder about entering the churches' political arena. Some *Gauleiters*, most notably Wilhelm Kube in Prussia, strove in 1931-1932 to gather Protestant support by infiltrating Nazi advocates into the parish councils. There were also positive responses from younger members of the Protestant clergy, especially those who championed a socially relevant form of Protestantism. In 1932 Pastor Joachim Hossenfelder founded the *Glaubensbewegung Deutsche Christen* which sought to forge a link between the national mission of the church and the political dynamism being shown by the Nazis.

That relationship seemed to be a natural outcome of the theological and political attitudes that had flourished among Evangelical-Protestants since the end of World War I. The conservative theological tone of Evangelical-Protestant life, particularly the theologians' readiness to include the nation among the orders of God-given creation, sustained an atmosphere that made the German Christian position seem plausible. It also gained credibility because the Protestant faithful's postwar sense of a profound national crisis deepened after 1929-1930. Many of them became reconciled to National Socialism because it appeared to be the vehicle of the national recovery for which they yearned. Their hope found support among such theologians as Wilhelm Stapel who abetted the appeal of the radical nationalist movement by identifying a *Volksnomos* which gave the nation a racial basis. Very few "New Lutheran" theologians went that far but their views had a degree of compatibility with an integral nationalism that made possible an early alignment between Evangelical-Protestants and National Socialism.

The alignment was inspired less by Nazi ideology than by the conviction that the church had to become associated with the national revolution in order to participate in its promise of a far-reaching national renewal. A large-scale German Christian movement came about only when the Nazis had gained their first great electoral success in 1930. An obligation to become involved helped to insure that one third of the votes cast in the 1932 Prussian synodal elections would go to the German Christians. By that date they controlled the church in Thuringia, an initial seat of Nazi political success.

How the churches fared after 1933 cannot be dealt with here. Out of the German Protestant churches' struggle with the Third Reich came an acknowledgment that the traditional political morality had to be revised. And further, that by cooperating with the Roman Catholics, the Christian electorate in Germany could form a great centrist, conservative political front.

Notes

1. More than thirty territorial churches in the German Empire, twenty-eight in the Weimar Republic and nineteen in the Federal Republic of (West) Germany. The *Evangelische Kirche in Deutschland* (1948) had more collective authority than any previous federation, but it diminished as a result of the division of Germany and the resurgence of the territorial churches.

2. James Luther Adams, "Rudolf Sohm's Theology of Law and Spirit," in Walter Leibrecht (ed.), *Religion and Culture: Essays in Honor of Paul Tillich* (New York, 1959), p. 233 and elsewhere.

3. The political mobilization had limits among the *Bildungsbürgertum* for whom politics remained an "unseemly activity." Arnold Brecht has testified that he had little interest in politics as a youth and as a university student (1902-1905). As a Justice Department assistant in Berlin (1906-1909) he took no interest in politics and had visited the Reichstag only once. His political concern awakened only with the outbreak of war in 1914. See Arnold Brecht, *The Political Education of Arnold Brecht. An Autobiography, 1884-1970* (Princeton, 1970), pp. 22, 33, and 59 ff.

4. See Wolfgand Treue (ed.), *Deutsche Parteiprogramme, 1861-1961* (3rd ed.; Göttingen, 1961), pp. 52-56.

5. A valuable survey is provided in Heinrich Bornkamm, *Luther im Spiegel der deutschen Geistesgeschichte* (2nd ed.; Göttingen, 1970).

6. Friedrich Naumann, *Demokratie und Kaisertum: Ein Handbuch für innere Politik* (4th ed.; Berlin-Schoneberg, 1905), which proposed that Germany should become a democratic caesarism, illustrated the growth of Protestant admiration and loyalty to the Reich and its chief of state.

7. That issue, first raised by Ernst Troeltsch and Friedrich Meinecke, is examined in Hajo Holborn, "German Idealism in the Light of German History," *Germany and Europe. Historical Essays by Hajo Holborn* (Garden City, New York, 1971), pp. 1-31. It was originally published in *Historische Zeitschrift*, CLXXIV (1952), 359-384.

8. Thus Adolf Schlatter, a "Biblical realist," had little influence before 1914. See his "Die Christenheit als politische Partei" (1914), in Karl Kupisch (ed.), *Quellen zur Geschichte des deutschen Protestantismus, 1871-1945* (Munich, 1960), pp. 110 ff.

THE HOLOCAUST:
THE LATENT ISSUE
IN THE UNIQUENESS DEBATE

John Murray Cuddihy

"There is no escape from the self-defeating ethos of exclusivism and intolerance...as long as our fundamental culture is
derived from a /Judeo-Christian/ religious tradition that
insists upon the dichotomous division of mankind into the
elect and the reprobate."

     —Richard L. Rubinstein, *The Cunning of History*:
The Holocaust and the American Future (New York, 1978),
p. 93.

"The problem...dealing with Jewish attitudes toward non-
Jews (*goyïm*) is the great sleeper issue of contemporary Jewish
life. It interacts with almost every aspect of the Jewish situation."

     —Michael Wyschogrod, "Love your (gentile)
Neighbor," *Sh'ma*, IX, No. 175 (May 25, 1979), 113.

STATEMENT TO MY READERS

1) Throughout, I am hardly ever speaking about the
Holocaust itself as an historical event. I am speaking about
speech about the Holocaust; I am talking about Holocaust
ideologies, about debates, and debates about the Holocaust.
Historiography, not history.

2) Even so, some of my ideas may offend. Nevertheless, I know this dread and awful murder occurred. It is a matter for grief as well as for study. I, too, grieve with Jews over their irreparable loss. And I too have been moved by the moral radiance of some of its victims. As I came to the end of Chaim Kaplan's *Warsaw Diary*, as the "destroyers" block by block closed in on him—yes, indeed, among them, 70 Jewish policemen, he notes with his usual bitter scrupulousness—and as I read his final words—"If my life ands—what will become of my diary?"—(I don't know what the common reaction is), I cried,—from sadness, from joy that the *Diary* and its testimony had survived in triumph, that a Pole had been its custodian, and that Kaplan had had the last word, for here was I, now, reading those very words, and crying.

I. Comparisons: "Obscene" or "Sacrilegious"?

The debate rages. It divides Jewish and Christian scholars, but, not infrequently, Jews and Christians can be found on both sides of the divide. *Is the Holocaust unique?* The argument runs right down into the very nomenclature for debating it. "What problems did the book /*Sophie's Choice*/ pose for you initially?" *LOOK* magazine asks author William Styron in the August issue. "There was a kind of sacrosanct quality about Auschwitz," he replies, "and from now on I'm going to say Auschwitz instead of the Holocaust because I'd prefer it. I fully understand the use of the word Holocaust, but I don't think it's applicable to the entire experience of the concentration camp, especially because it applies to a lot of other people who were not Jewish who were victims. So I'm going to use Auschwitz as a generic description," he concludes bluntly. [1]

The argument *for* the uniqueness of the Holocaust, on the other hand, occurs, frequently, in oblique form, in the indignant denial of the legitimacy of comparison, or in the brusque dismissal, say, of the Armenian massacre as an "obscene comparison." City University of New York historian Henry Feingold, for example, criticizes Marcel Ophuls, film director of "The Meaning of Justice," for his tendency to rob the Jewish Holocaust of its "horrendous particularity" and thus to "trivialize" it. "Nazism becomes not a *uniquely* demonic force," he writes, "but the dark side of the human spirit which lurks in all of us." [2] The comparisons and equations Daniel Ellsberg formulates in this same film represent an attempt, Dorothy Rabinowitz claims, "to discredit the idea of a *unique* evil perpetrated by Nazism and unequaled in history." [3]

Why do so many Jewish and some Gentile scholars insist on the uniqueness of the Holocaust? The obvious first answer is: because it *was* unique. The obvious reply to this is: but every event in any region of space-time is unique. The answer to this, in turn, is given by Roy Eckhardt: but the Holocaust is "uniquely unique." [4]

"Uniquely unique" according to what criterion, in what category? There has been much search — research — invested in establishing such a criterion, a criterion that will be positive and not negative, empirical and not mystical, one which will decisively differentiate the Holocaust from all other atrocities and from all other genocides. A quantitative criterion, since scale is a continuous variable, will not do, since it invites, precisely, comparison. The quarry of this quest is for a property which will place the Holocaust in a *sui generis* category.

Paul Robinson, in the *New York Times Book Review*, in questioning Bruno Bettleheim's conviction that our age has been uniquely terrible and that its unique terribleness found perfect expression in the death camps of the Third Reich, examines three explanations typically advanced for the uniqueness of the Holocaust: it was systematic or total, it was senseless or non-instrumental, and it was specifically death-intending. Each criterion is, in the end, found wanting. But what really troubles Robinson is not the inadequacy of the various criteria, but the search for a category of uniqueness itself. "It serves little intellectual or moral purpose, in my opinion, to insist that the victims of the camps occupy a status ontologically different from, say, the victims of Alexander the Great, Attila the Hun, the Albigensian Crusade, the Thirty Years' War, European imperialism or black slavery." The reason given for "placing the destruction of European Jewry in a distinct category" are important, "but they do not categorically separate the holocaust /sic/ from other historical acts of humanity." Of course there are distinct differences between, say, "the horrors of the holocaust and those of slavery" but "we should resist the temptation to make the distinction categorical." [5]

If we listen carefully to this text "with the third ear," do we not hear echoes of the Jesus Prayer, "...lead us not into temptation?" By yielding to the temptation to make the difference between the Holocaust and, for example, slavery categorical, Robinson continues, "we do not deepen our sense of shame about what we, as a species, have done to one another. Just the opposite: We impoverish that sense because we dismiss as relatively trivial all the sins that mankind has to answer for up to 1933." A further consequence: "one would have to set aside as out-of-date the great historical portrayals of human wickedness left to us by, among others, Dante, Shakespeare and Milton, for the simple reason that there was no holocaust in the moral universe of any of these artists." [6]

In the "temptation" to make the Holocaust *sui generis* Robinson detects a sin, the sin of "impoverishing" our sense of shame and guilt by particularizing it. He urges that we "resist" that temptation.

Let us turn now to the other side. How do Jewish proponents of the utter, unique depravity of the Holocaust hear comparisons between the Holocaust and other atrocities? Let us attend to Professor Michael Walzer of Harvard. Walzer listens as Yehudi Menuhin, in the Ophuls film, says, ' "Every human being is guilty...' " /of the Holocaust/, and Walzer's instant reaction is: "That is a pleasantly Christian pronouncement...." [7] I think that in this text we must take the adjective "Christian" as importantly as in Robinson's case we took words like "resisting," "temptation," and "sin." The unmistakably sardonic undertone of Walzer's words is inseparable from the conviction that, in Menuhin, he confronts a Jew who, tempted to apostasize from the uncomfortable particularity of Jewish identity and the Holocaust, has succumbed to the lure of a "pleasant" Christian universalism.

Another argument for the uniqueness and centrality of the Jewish victims in World War II is the well-known argument from "reversed" priorities of Lucy Dawidowicz and others. The idea that Nazi anti-Semitism was of "a

qualitatively different character than its predecessors in
central Europe and that it held a unique primacy in Nazi
decision-making is not a new one," as historian Henry Feingold notes, citing Poliakov, Mosse, and Jacob Robinson.
Instances of the diversion of rolling stock and personnel from
prosecuting the physical or national war to the ideological
"war against the Jews" do not prove that the ideological war
against the Jews was necessarily the real or primary war.
Feingold writes:

> The absence of even a pretense of being value free
> history raises questions on the nature of the evidence
> Dawidowicz used to prove the primacy of the war
> against the Jews.... For Jews and their historians
> the holocaust is naturally the touchstone of all
> sensibility. But does that distort a true historical
> perspective? Ethnocentric readings are not un-
> heard of among Jewish historians.... To my
> knowledge no noteworthy student of European
> history would deny that a racial fixation was one
> of the keys to Nazi motivation, but neither would
> any of them assign to the Nazis' racial ideology
> the role that Dawidowicz does....the liquidation
> of the Jews, terrible as it was, was a relatively minor
> happening. Genocide is neither unprecedented
> nor metahistorical. The 'final solution,' /Feingold
> concludes/, takes its place with other atrocities in
> the bloody history of the West. Seen on the larger
> canvas of European history, the holocaust does
> not have the importance and uniqueness it has
> on the canvas of Jewish history. [8]

Even if the argument from "reversed" priorities or
counterproductivity were to prove the priority of the fanatical ideological war against the Jews, this would not of itself
categorically distinguish the Holocaust from the Armenian
genocide. For example, Helen Fein in her recent, powerful book, *Accounting for Genocide*, notes that the German
Ambassador to Turkey, Count Wolf-Metternich, "understood that the Armenian extermination was an end in itself
to the ruling /Turkish/ triumvirate and its party...," and
quotes the ambassador's complaint that the Turkish ally,
in its efforts to deport and exterminate the Armenians,

" 'hampers the conduct of the war. These measures...gave the impression as if the Turkish government were itself bent on losing the war.' " Professor Fein, noting that "skilled Jewish workers were killed and railroad cars were diverted to bring the Final Solution into effect rather than to mobilize against the allies," adds, "just as Armenian workers had been annihilated in Turkey during World War I, hindering Turkey's mobilization." [9]

Emil Fackenheim, a philosopher of the Holocaust, defends a version of the centrality thesis in arguing for uniqueness. Refusing what he takes to be Richard Rubenstein's "extreme technological nightmare" analysis of the Holocaust, that, he maintains, derives from Lewis Mumford and others, in which the Jews become the "waste products" of a radically dehumanized industrial machine, [10] Fackenheim identifies the uniqueness of the Holocaust with the uniqueness of its victims: it was uniquely and directly targeted to Jews.

The text in which he summarizes his conclusion bears close reading: "We must conclude, then," he writes, "that the dead Jews of the murder camps /and here Fackenheim adds a revealing parenthetical aside/ (and all other innocent victims, as it were, as quasi-Jews, or by dint of innocent-guilt-by-association) were not the 'waste product' of the Nazi system. They were *the* product." [11]

The Gypsies, Catholic Poles, Christian Slavs, and others are proving to be syntactically awkward for this particular reading of the Holocaust, just as they proved to be juridically awkward, as we shall see, during the Eichmann trial in Jerusalem. If the uniqueness of the Holocaust is demonstrated by the uniqueness of its victims—the Jews—then the *other* victims become a kind of residue, to be mentioned in passing in a parenthesis, and converted to a new, and sociologically anomalous, if presumably honorable, status: "quasi-Jews," "as if Jews." "It helps, even if we are not ourselves victims, if we can 'claim relationship with' accredited victims." [12]

The Gentile victims at Auschwitz, then, become what Talcott Parsons calls a "residual category," whose deaths were somehow the unintended consequences of a purposeful social action, who died as if they were not themselves but stand-ins for another group, the Jews.

Fackenheim's *als ob* strategy for coping parataxically with the Gypsy and Gentile victims of Auschwitz involves a curious sequel. Two years later, in early June of 1974, a Jewish and Christian symposium on Auschwitz was held at the Cathedral Church of St. John the Divine in New York City. [13] Eighteen days later there appeared, on the Op-Ed page of *The New York Times*, an essay by the novelist William Styron, in which he protested the symposium's "overwhelming emphasis on anti-Semitism and Christian guilt." Noting that more than one million Christian Slavs were murdered in the same way as the Jews, in the same place, he concluded: "...I cannot accept anti-Semitism as the sole touchstone by which we examine the monstrous paradigm that Auschwitz has become...to place all the blame on Christian theology is to ignore the complex secular roots of anti-Semitism as well.... If /the Holocaust/ was anti-Semitic," he ends, "it was also anti-Christian...it was anti-human. Anti-life." [14]

Styron's reaction to the Auschwitz symposium provoked, in turn, the notoriously indignant and astonishing counter-attack by Cynthia Ozick, "A Liberal's Auschwitz." (It appeared, in a quarterly appropriately titled *Confrontation*.) In this reply of Ozick, defending the uniqueness of the Holocaust, Fackenheim's quasi-victims return, minus their parenthesis. "The Jews," Ozick retorts to Styron, "were not an *instance* of Nazi slaughter; they were the purpose and whole reason for it. Like any successful factory in roaring production," she adds, "the German death-factory produced useful by-products: the elimination of Slavs and most Gypsies." [15]

A curious transposition occurs in this Ozick text. In the original Fackenheim formulation, which Ozick had evidently read, [16] the term "waste product" is vigorously rejected as applicable to Jewish victims. Ozick then picks up the epithet rejected by Fackenheim for Jews, changes it to "by-product," and applies it to the non-Jews.

In this Ozickian hermeneutic of the Holocaust, Christian Slavs and most Gypsies are, indeed, *de facto* victims, but they fail to achieve what I have elsewhere called "accredited victim" status. [17] They fail to achieve it because, being an ascriptive status, it *cannot* be achieved. For Miss Ozick these "non-Jewish" victims are dead all right, but dead for all the wrong reasons, incidentally dead, mere "by-products" of the Holocaust, as she calls them, lapsing into her revealing and ghastly metaphor.

Styron waits three years and then returns to the thrust of Ozick's "by-product" metaphor in a *New York Review of Books* essay entitled "Hell Reconsidered." [18] He argues as follows: Yes, he concedes, the vast numbers of Russians, Polish Christians, Gypsies, and others who were exterminated by the Nazis "would possibly seem less meaningful if the victims had been part of the mere detritus of war, accidental casualties, helpless *by-products* of the Holocaust; but such was not the case...." [19]

II. Residual Categories, Like Ideas, Have Consequences

Hovering over the uniqueness debate as we look back, and haunting it at every turn, there is, I believe, an ancient residual category, viz., that of "non-Jew." It re-emerges at all the great turning points in Jewish history, and in all the great historiographical debates: in the Balfour Declaration, during the Eichmann trial, in the historiography of the Holocaust. Residual categories are negative categories, and they create not only substantive and methodological problems for the social scientist but they have moral consequences for human beings.

The late Talcott Parsons offered this definition of a residual category (in *The Structure of Social Action*)—be thinking of the category "non-Jew" as you read it:

> If, as is almost always the case, not all the actually observable facts of the field, or those which have been observed, fit into the sharply, positively defined categories, they tend to be given one or more blanket names which refer to categories negatively defined, that is, of facts known to exist, which are even more or less adequately described, but are defined theoretically by their failure to fit into the positively defined categories of the system. The only theoretically significant statements that can be made about these facts are negative statements—they are *not* so and so. [20]

Let us take two examples, the Balfour Declaration and the Eichmann trial.

When British foreign secretary Arthur James (subsequently Lord) Balfour, at the instigation of Chaim Weizmann and Nahum Sokolow, wrote his famous 67-word letter to the second Baron Rothschild on November 2, 1917, the two sleeper words among the 67 were "home" and "non-Jewish": "...His Majesty's Government view with favour the establishment in Palestine of a national *home* for the Jewish people, ...it being clearly understood that nothing shall be done which may prejudice the civil and religious rights of existing *non-Jewish* communities in Palestine...." [21] The population of Palestine at the time was 800,000, of which 58,000 were Jews. [22] The "non-Jewish" population category was 742,000. With the vast majority of Palestinians thus defined residually, as not being Jews, it was understandable that Herzl could speak of the Jews as "a people without a land" emigrating to "a land without a people."

In the Eichmann trial, in the eleventh count of the indictment, Eichmann was convicted of the "deportation" of "scores of thousands of Gypsies" to Auschwitz, but he was not also convicted of their murder by the Israeli court, as he was in the case of Jewish victims. Hannah Arendt comments on this as follows: "...the judgement /of the court/ held that 'it has not been proved before us that the accused knew that the Gypsies were being transported to destruction'—which meant," Arendt notes, "that no genocide charge except the 'crime against the Jewish people' was brought" in the Eichmann trial. [23]

The court, Arendt appears to be arguing, embraced the defendant's own alibi—namely, Eichmann's fiction of the separation of deportation from extermination—only when it applied to the Gypsies. For how is the Holocaust to be uniquely Jewish unless a way can be found for juridically confining the crime of genocide uniquely to its Jewish victims?

> This was difficult to understand /Arendt remarks/,
> for, apart from the fact that the extermination of
> the Gypsies was common knowledge, Eichmann had
> admitted during the police interrogation that he
> knew of it.... His department had been commission-

ed to undertake the 'evacuation' of thirty thousand
Gypsies from Reich territory, and he could not remember the details very well, because there had
been no intervention from any side; but that the
Gypsies, like Jews, were shipped off to be exterminated he had never doubted. /Thus/ he was guilty
of their extermination /she concludes/, in exactly
the same way he was guilty of the extermination
of the Jews. [24]

Before concluding this section, we will take one more
text for analysis. In his second Stroum lecture, "Against
Mystification: The Holocaust as a Historical Phenomenon," Professor Yehuda Bauer of Hebrew University,
while conceding that there are certain parallels to the
Holocaust—otherwise "the whole phenomenon is inexpli-
cable" [25] —insists at the same time on the utter uniqueness
of the Jewish situation. What is significant for us is that he
falls back on two lexicons to argue this position: Marxist
and religious.

"Not to see the difference...," he writes, "not to realize
that the Jewish situation was unique, is to mystify history," [26]
and he sets his task as the demystification of the mystification. But soon, significantly, he builds to the language of
classical, Levitical anathema: "...to say that the Holocaust
is the total of all the crimes committed by Nazism in Europe,
to do any or all of this is an inexcusable *abomination*...." [27]

Despite his book's title, *The Holocaust in Historical
Perspective,* Bauer culminates with a definition of the Holocaust in the perspective of religion, religious not alone from
the perspective of the victims but, surprisingly, from the
perspective of the perpetrators also: "Holocaust," he writes,
"was the policy of the total, *sacral* Nazi act of mass murder
of all Jews they could lay hands on." [28]

There is, this suggests, a latent sacred interpretation of
the Holocaust that surfaces from time to time, even in academic Jews of impeccable secularity. It is as though the ultimate, evidential proof of the Holocaust's uniqueness had to
pass through a process of radically separating one class of
Hitler's victims from all the others before appealing to the
intention of Hitler himself as a guarantee, when empirical
doubts arise, of the centrality of the class of Jewish victims.

When all else fails, we can fall back on the fanatical purity of Hitler's racial fixation: He, at least, knew what he was doing. Others of us may be misled by trivial comparisons with other carnage; Hitler alone discerned the unique identity of his sacred victim.

Bauer's definition, like Ozick's, validates this eerie latent hermeneutic of the Holocaust. The ultimate, hidden assumption behind the insistent definition of the Holocaust as "uniquely unique"—from Bauer to Eckhardt—involves essentially a Durkheimian division of the Holocaust "product"—its victims—into two kinds: sacred and profane. Thus, to call the Nazi Holocaust, as Bauer does, a "sacral Nazi act," may be—if we may think the unthinkable—to depict Hitler himself as beholden to the Orthodox Jewish definition of itself as a sacred people, a people apart, a *goy kadosh?* a people *k'khol ha-goyim* that, even in death, is forbidden to mingle with "the nations," with what Cynthia Ozick calls the unintended or profane consequences, the mere "by-products," the—dare we say it?—*trayf* of the "sacral" act of Holocaust? [29] Two ritual categories of victim: the "sacred," intended victims, and the profane "by-products": is this not—as Robie Macauley says [30] —a way of playing Hitler's game?

Or *is* it? Suppose Hitler borrowed his game. [31] Who started this game anyway? Who cares?! The point is to stop playing it. As Richard Rubenstein writes: "There is no escape from the self-defeating ethos of exclusivism and intolerance...as long as our fundamental culture is derived from a /Judeo-Christian/ religious tradition that insists upon the dichotomous division of mankind into the elect and the reprobate." [32]

III. Symbols of Subcultural Status: Prestige as a Control
     System

Whatever the merits of the uniqueness claim, we can still inquire into its functions. Even if our contention as to the latent content of the uniqueness debate—viz., that the uniqueness claim is premised on a secularized (and sometimes not so secularized) conviction of Jewish chosenness—should prove to be inadequate or false, as sociologists we can still examine what functions (latent and manifest) the claim to the Holocaust's uniqueness performs for its claimants.

One function, for example, is that by stressing what I have called "sacred particularity," [33] empirical enquiry into the complex *secular* roots of anti-Semitism is neglected in favor of easy theological deductions. A direct causal emanation from the cultural value system into the social system spares us the trouble of seeing what conditions in politics, economics, demography, and psychology conduce to anti-Semitism.

Again, the uniqueness claim lends itself to the classical Zionist ideological conviction of the ubiquity and eternity of Diaspora anti-Semitism. A unique Holocaust involves the almost *a priori* symbiosis of Judaism and anti-Semitism. This interpretation claims, according to David Blumenthal, that the Holocaust, "in its truest sense, is a Jewish affair; that it, *therefore*, has its deepest roots in anti-Semitism.... It is more than ironic that both the Zionists and their enemies should perceive the hermeneutic of the Holocaust developed by the Jewish community as being the same." [34] "In this connection," Peter Berger argues, "the insistence by some that the Holocaust must be the core of Jewish self-reflection today has the *function* of freezing the presence of anti-Semitism in the consciousness of Jews—and thus covering up the question of why one should be a Jew." [35] Berger calls this insistence a "strategy" for circumventing the "heretical imperative" of choice immanent in modernity. [36]

My chief interest in the uniqueness claim is to ask: What, today, is the Jewish community getting out of this claim? What function is the consuming interest in the Holocaust performing for the Jewish subculture and its members? Like all important, deep concerns, even obsessions, this one is "overdetermined," sociologically speaking. It has many functions to perform, and more than one reason for existing.

I select, as the focus of my interest, the Holocaust and its uniqueness claim as an instance of a cultural status claim. Too often, status is seen in relation to social class alone. My work has explored how subcultures and their minority intellectuals may be viewed as *cultural* status-seekers engaged in an inter-ethnic and intra-societal *kulturkampf*.

Like the struggle of scientists over priorities in scientific discovery—which Robert Merton has so brilliantly explored [37] —I view the ardent concern for uniqueness as a special case of what Merton calls "the power of the drive for ethnocentric esteem." [38] What he terms "the type of ethnocentric concern with national priority of discovery that turns up again and again...," [39] I regard as a variant form of the concern with uniqueness or specialness. Let us be frank: National priority and national uniquity (uniqueness) are both covert claims to superiority, parallel paths to the same summit, and that summit is what Merton calls "ethnocentric glory." [40] Individuals, like groups, pursue the prestige of the superiority of uniqueness even in the terrible passages of their history. "Jesus Christ, *supreme* victim" [41] may be a paradox; it is not a contradiction.

As in the case of "Symbols of Class Status," as Goffman has shown, [42] so in the case of symbols of cultural (and subcultural) status, uniqueness is a pre-eminent cultural value, enabling cultures (and subcultures), and the groups which are their carriers to be invidiously ranked on a scale of prestige.

Of course, much Holocaust attention is a prolonged act of grieving. It is grief-work. [43] Some interest in the Holocaust is sheer cognitive desire to know for-its-own-sake "what happened?" Another of its functions is to memorialize, to remember, and at the same time—perhaps paradoxically— to celebrate. There is a genuine effort to participate in—to use the title of William Goode's recent study—*The Celebration of Heroes*, to which we must add his more sociological subtitle: *Prestige As a Control System.*[44]

To the profane eyes of a sociologist who is neither a Jew nor a Christian, one of the obvious if latent functions of the appeal to a sacred uniqueness is that it stakes out a subcultural status claim to exclusiveness, setting the claimant's group and its members apart and making them immune from comparison. Praising the superiority of one's group becomes a legitimate avenue of indirect self-congratulation. Self-regarding sentiment, improper as egoism, is praiseworthy when it acts out as "us-ism."

In good part, the status power of the Holocaust symbol derives from the fact that it functions as a double theodicy: in one act, it separates Jews from Gentiles and blames Gentiles, in the person of Hitler, for that separation. This is the function of the uniqueness claim that Jacob Neusner of Brown University has in mind when he writes of the Holocaust not as an historical event, but as an ideology, the Holocaust in italics. Neusner writes: " 'The Holocaust' is the Jews' special thing: it is what sets them apart from others while giving them a claim upon those others. That is why," Neusner concludes, "Jews insist on the 'uniqueness of the Holocaust.' " [45] What Neusner calls "the claim upon others" that the Holocaust confers is what I call the social control function exercised by the prestige of cultural and subcultural symbols. Like social class symbols, cultural symbols serve "to influence in a desired direction other persons' judgment" of the group that is the symbol's carrier. [46] Think of the aristocratic function of family trees and "patents" of nobility. Symbolic cultural behavior, or social action featuring symbols, is designed to move (and thus to socially control) others, to pay us the old difficult *doxa*: glory, honor, praise, esteem, approval, deference, opinion, repute. The craving for recognition and prestige is ubiquitous. How, when legal sanctions do not apply, prevent the misrepresentative use of class and cultural symbols? A latent function of at least some of the research devoted to the Holocaust symbol is to find, in the absence of *legal* restrictions for the misrepresentative use of it, moral, intrinsic, natural, socialization, and cultivation restrictions [47] on the misuse of it.

It is in this light that one should view even the definitional struggle itself, in its focus on uniqueness. Uniqueness is at once a device for conferring status and for preventing "fraud" (i.e., "obscene comparisons"). Hence, cultural items, events, and behavior used to signify cultural prestige — paralleling the case of class and social status — are frequently proposed and defended on the basis of limited supply or natural scarcity. What Goffman calls "historical closure" [48] is a form of temporal scarcity. An incident a few years back illustrates the importance of this as a device for restricting misrepresentative use of the Holocaust symbol.

The late Shlomo Katz, then editor of *Midstream* magazine, got into an angry exchange with black novelist-intellectual James Baldwin over Baldwin's comparison of the solitariness of prisoner Angela Davis to that of "the Jewish

housewife on the way to Dachau." "Everybody," he wrote
indignantly, "tries to jump on each other's bandwagon without regard to fact, to meaning, to consequence...." Then
Katz proceeded to instruct Baldwin in the fact "that genocide has happened, once and for all, in the literal sense,
and not in the rhetorical misuse of it 'by fly-by-night self-
styled revolutionaries.' " It is the term "fly-by-night" that
gives the game away; Katz "considers himself to be addressing, clearly, cultural upstarts" who, in a subcultural status
struggle, are violating proprietary cultural rights in a pre-
cious and unique symbol. [49] In the status-politics of subcultures, emulation is experienced as subversion, as, in another institution of the culture system, the art world, supreme
value attaches to "originals," not "reproductions."

The case of Katz and Baldwin is an early example of
the genus "obscene comparison" which Katz seeks to inter-
dict by the device of "historical closure." Professor Yehuda
Bauer, on the other hand, while insisting on historical
uniqueness, shades the position, writing: "We should prop-
erly use the term 'Holocaust' to describe the policy of total
annihilation of a nation or a people," adding: *To date*,
this has happened once, to the Jews under Nazism." [50] This
is a modified "historical closure" position.

In part to prevent misuse of the cultural (or class) symbol,
a curator personnel of subcultural intellectuals emerges
"whose task it is to build and service" [51] the symbol (or
symbols) of cultural status. A cultural control system devel-
ops to prevent symbol contamination — religiously, syncretism — and to monitor and expose the evasions and circum-
ventions of the devices for restricting misrepresentable uses
of the Holocaust symbol. These curator groups seek to prevent what William Goode calls the "subversion of the prestige
process." [52]

In such "subversion" through imitation, comparison,
and, occasionally, outright falsification, other groups seize
and manipulate the symbol for their own purposes. A form
of such "subversion" occurs when the privileged symbol cir-
culates [53] downward — call this "vulgarization" — or outward
to other groups — call this "expropriation" by another group
(say Blacks) — or upward — call this "elevation" (or universal-
ization).

The drive behind the uniqueness claim—in this perspective, that of subcultural status aspirations—is to place the symbol "beyond comparison," as, for example, when people exclaim: "Oh, there's no comparison!"

This exemption from comparison is a heady privilege. This very exemption is itself a symbol of high cultural *yichus*. Among the many items selected by culture to symbolize status, incomparability alone is inimitable.

Notes

1. Peter H. Stone, "A Conversation with William Styron," *LOOK*, n.s., II, No. 2 (August, 1979), 34.

2. Henry Feingold, "Ophuls 'The Meaning of Justice': The Power and the Muddle," *Congress Monthly*, XLIII, No. 8 (October, 1976), 8 (my italics).

3. Dorothy Rabinowitz, "Ophuls: Justice Misremembered," *Commentary*, LXII, No. 6 (December, 1976), 67 (my italics).

4. A. Roy Eckhardt, "Is the Holocaust Unique?" *Worldview*, XVII, No. 9 (September, 1974), 31.

5. Paul Robinson, "Apologist for the Superego" /review of Bruno Bettleheim, *Surviving and Other Essays*/, *The New York Times Book Review*, April 29, 1979, p. 63.

6. *Ibid*.

7. Michael Walzer, "The Memory of Justice: Marcel Ophuls and the Nuremberg Trials," *The New Republic*, LXXV, No. 15 (October 9, 1976), 21.

8. Henry L. Feingold /review of Lucy Dawidowicz, *The War against the Jews, 1933-1945* (New York, 1975)/, *Jewish Social Studies*, XXXVIII, No. 1 (1976), 83.

9. Helen Fein, *Accounting for Genocide: National Responses and Jewish Victimization during the Holocaust* (New York, 1979), pp. 16-17, 24.

10. Emil L. Fackenheim, "The Human Condition after Auschwitz: A Jewish Testimony a Generation After," *Congress Bi-Weekly*, XXXIX, No. 7 (April 28, 1972), 9.

11. *Ibid*., p. 10, reprinted in Emil L. Fackenheim, *The Jewish Return into History: Reflections in the Age of Auschwitz and a New Jerusalem* (New York, 1978), p. 93.

12. John Murray Cuddihy, *The Ordeal of Civility: Freud, Marx, Levi-Strauss, and the Jewish Struggle with Modernity* (New York, 1974), p. 212.

13. The papers are collected in Eva Fleischner (ed.), *Auschwitz: Beginning of a New Era? Reflections on the Holocaust* (New York, 1977).

14. William Styron, "Auschwitz's Message," *The New York Times*, June 25, 1974, p. 37.

15. Cynthia Ozick, "A Liberal's Auschwitz," *Confrontation*, No. 10 (Spring, 1975), 128.

16. This is extrinsically probable because — among other reasons — Ozick was herself a much-discussed author in the pages of the *Congress Bi-Weekly*. In the next issue, e.g., carrying the concluding Part II of Fackenheim's essay (May 19, 1974), she is singled out for prominent mention twice (24 and 30). Again in the very next issue (June 30, 1972), a reviewer writes that "Cynthia Ozick has called attention to..." etc. (25).

17. Cuddihy, *Ordeal of Civility...*, p. 212.

18. Part of this article reappears in altered form as the "Introduction" by William Styron to Richard L. Rubenstein, *The Cunning of History: The Holocaust and the American Future* (New York, 1978). / The book is a paperback edition of *The Cunning of History: Mass Death and the American Future* (New York, 1975)/.

19. William Styron, "Hell Reconsidered," *The New York Review of Books*, XXV, No. 11 (June 29, 1978), 12 (my italics).

20. Talcott Parsons, *The Structure of Social Action: A Study in Social Theory with Special Reference to a Group of Recent European Writers* (Glencoe, Illinois, 1949), pp. 17-18. For another application of this concept, see Cuddihy, *Ordeal of Civility...*, p. 222.

21. Howard Morley Sachar, *The Course of Modern Jewish History* (New York, 1958), p. 375 (my italics).

22. Cecil Roth, *A History of the Jews* (New York, 1961), p. 375.

23. Hannah Arendt, *Eichmann in Jerusalem: A Report on the Banality of Evil* (New York, 1964), p. 245.

24. *Ibid.* The word "Thus" appears in the earlier *The New Yorker* version.

25. Yehuda Bauer, *The Holocaust in Historical Perspective* (Seattle, 1978), p. 36.

26. *Ibid.*

27. *Ibid.*, pp. 37, 38 (my italics).

28. *Ibid.*, p. 36 (my italics).

29. For a different development of this theme — the secularization of Jewish chosenness — see Chap. 5, "Rabbi Arthur Hertzberg and the Metaphoricality of Jewish Chosenness" in John Murray Cuddihy, *No Offense: Civil Religion and Protestant Taste* (New York, 1978), pp. 101-155.

30. "Letters to the Editor: Who Should Mourn?", *The New York Times Book Review*, August 8, 1976, p. 22.

31. See the *"Erster Punkt"* in George Steiner, "The Portage to San Christobal of A. H.," *The Kenyon Review*, n.s., I, No. 2 (Spring, 1979), 114-116.

32. Rubenstein, *Cunning of History...* (1978), p. 93.

33. Cf. Cuddihy, *Ordeal of Civility...*, p. 235.

34. David R. Blumenthal, "Scholarly Approaches to the Holocaust," *SHOAH*, I, No. 3 (Winter, 1979), 23 (my italics).

35. Peter L. Berger, "Converting the Gentiles," *Commentary*, LXVII, No. 5 (May, 1979), 36 (my italics).

36. Cf. Peter L. Berger, *The Heretical Imperative: Contemporary Possibilities of Religious Affirmation* (Garden City, New York, 1979).

37. Cf. Robert K. Merton in Norman W. Storer (ed.), *The Sociology of Science: Theoretical and Empirical Investigations* (Chicago and London, 1973), Chap. 14.

38. *Ibid.*, p. 184.

39. *Ibid.*

40. *Ibid.*, p. 185.

41. Cf. Cuddihy, *Ordeal of Civility...*, p. 212.

42. Erving Goffman, "Symbols of Class Status," *The British Journal of Sociology*, II (1951), 294-304. I will quote from the reprint in Howard Robboy *et al.* (eds.), *Social Interaction: Introductory Readings in Sociology* (New York, 1979), pp. 266-276.

43. Cf. Peter Marris, *Loss and Change* (New York, 1974).

44. Berkeley, 1978.

45. Jacob Neusner, "A 'Holocaust' Primer," *National Review*, XXXI, No. 31 (August 3, 1979), 978.

46. Goffman, "Symbols...," in Robboy *et al.* (eds.), *Social Interaction...*, p. 268.

47. *Ibid.*, pp. 269-272.

48. *Ibid.*, p. 270.

49. All these passages are in Cuddihy, *Ordeal of Civility...*, p. 211.

50. Yehuda Bauer, *The Holocaust...*, p. 38 (my italics).

51. Goffman, "Symbols...," p. 274.

52. William J. Goode, *The Celebration of Heroes: Prestige as a Social Control System* (Berkeley, 1978). See Chap. 10: "The Dynamics of Subversion."

53. Goffman, "Symbols...," p. 274.

THE HOSPITALLERS OF RHODES CONFRONT THE TURKS: 1306-1421*

Anthony Luttrell

Religion may play a variety of roles in confrontations between groups belonging to different faiths. The religious attitudes involved may be zealous and enthusiastic or merely formal, while motives are seldom unmixed, and the existence of economic or material objectives need not exclude elements of genuine fervor; ideological conflicts are frequently accompanied by contradictions and ambiguities.

The Turcoman or Turkic peoples whom the Latin Hospitallers faced from the offshore island of Rhodes after they had conquered it between 1306 and 1310 were relatively new Muslims whose language was not Arabic. They belonged to groups which had for several centuries been moving from central Asia into Anatolia, pushing back Byzantine rule and gradually attracting the indigenous populations to Islam. The Seljuk sultanate which they set up was subsequently overcome by Mongol invaders, after which nomadic or quasi-nomadic tribal groupings or emirates emerged, some of them occupying the Aegean coastlands after about 1270 and beginning to assemble their own naval forces. Opposite Rhodes was the Emirate of Menteshe; further north, along the Maeander Valley, were the Emirs of Aiden; and beyond them were others, including the Ottomans. The successful development of these groups certainly owed something to the appeal of their *ghazi* ethos and to their invocation of a holy war. Yet these nomadic tribal leaders regularly attacked each other, allied with Christians and served them as mercenaries or accepted regular annual tributes from them; furthermore, they fought for plunder and pas-

ture, absorbed, but made little attempt to convert, the
Christian peasants of Anatolia, encouraged and taxed Latin
commerce in their own lands, and on occasions might even
have followed non-Islamic practices such as human sacrifice
or horse worship.[1]

At the same time Turkish naval forces were launching
razzias against the Aegean islands and raiding parts of the
Greek mainland. The Turks certainly regarded the Latins
as enemies and despised them as infidels. Muslim preachers
and teachers were establishing themselves in the increasingly sedentary and bureaucratic centers of the emirates,
providing a compelling ideology for religious conflict and
and incitement to plunder. Ibn Battuta, who travelled extensively through western Anatolia in about 1331, found
holy men, legists, and religious colleges in many of the larger
towns he passed through.[2] Later he was to describe Umur
of Aidin as a "pious prince" who was "continually engaged
in *jihad* or holy war," who raided and plundered the
Christians, who repeatedly seized booty and prisoners, and
who died a "martyr's death" while attacking the Latins at
Smyrna in 1348.[3] An inscription of 1337 at Bursa concerning Osman's son Orhkan called him "warrior of the holy
war...Sultan of the *ghazis, ghazi* son of *ghazi*, hero of
the world and of the faith..."."[4]

* * *

Despite its original charitable and hospitaller functions,
the Order of Saint John developed into a primarily warlike
institution, one of a group of Christian, Latin military orders
which emerged after the First Crusade. Their development
and mentality were conditioned by the religious war which
had been fought first to acquire and protect the sacred
places at Jerusalem, and later to defend the Latin presence
in Syria. Like the *jihad*, the crusade was dependent upon
powerful religious impulses, but it too had its materialistic
aspects, its expansionist and commercial overtones, and its
conquests, massacres, and pillagings. The crusading machine
was also turned against Greek schismatics and Latin heretics, and was used to combat the Christian enemies of the
pope in Italy and elsewhere in the West. It provided the
papacy with an opportunity to exercise a political leader-

ship, to raise clerical taxation from crusading tenths, and, more crudely, to sell crusade indulgences.

Like many other orders, whether military, monastic, mendicant, charitable, or otherwise, the Hospital was a society of religious whose members took permanent, lifelong vows of poverty, chastity, and obedience, who followed a rule and statutes confirmed by their ultimate superior the pope, and who lived a liturgical life of communal prayer. The Hospitaller brethren, never very numerous, belonged to different classes: a dominant minority of knights or *milites* whose numbers dwindled late in the fourteenth century; *sergentes*, a small number of fighting men of lesser social rank; a considerable group of priests; and a variety of sisters, donats, *confratres*, and lay associates. The Hospitallers had a military function, being dedicated to warfare against the infidel; they were not permitted to bear arms against fellow Christians. Across the centuries they had been endowed by numerous rulers and other individual donors with extensive properties, privileges, and exemptions in the West, and they were morally and politically obliged to justify these advantageous benefits with demonstrably warlike activity against the infidel. [5] Paradoxically, the Hospital's unceasing struggle, whether it involved active operations or watchful garrison duties, was not a crusade, that is, an occasional and chronologically-limited event constituted by and dependent on a papal proclamation. Furthermore, while an individual became a crusader by vowing himself to a single crusading expedition and not for a lifetime of service, the Hospitaller, though he wore a cross in memory of Christ and his suffering, could not take the crusading cross because he had sworn a vow of obedience and could not make other vows. In fact, a series of papal bulls conceded that a Hospitaller who died fighting against the infidel would enjoy the same spiritual benefits or indulgences as if he were himself a crusader. [6]

During the thirteenth century the Hospital developed as an efficient military geared to mercenary auxiliary forces and strong defensible stone castles, with a support system based on a continual influx of men and money from the West. When the defense of Syria came to a close with the fall of Acre in 1310, the two major military orders retired to Cyprus, their fighting manpower decimated and demoralized, and their Syrian incomes and possessions entirely lost. Western opinion blamed them for the collapse of the crusade, and certain rulers coveted or feared their wealth. The military orders faced a crisis of identity and determination. The Teutonic brethren transferred their headquarters from Venice to Marienbad in Prussia in 1309. The Templars dithered and involved themselves in debatable financial manipulations and Cypriot dynastic politics; the French king attacked them in 1307 and the pope dissolved their order in 1312. In 1306 the Hospitallers, still based on Cyprus under conditions which cramped their possibilities of action and lacking any naval strength, needed to display a clear intention to combat the infidel. By invading Rhodes they saved themselves from the possible consequences of serious criticism.[7]

The conquest of Rhodes was an obscure and ambiguous operation. Together with certain Genoese piratical adventurers, the Hospitallers attacked a Christian island which formed part of schismatic Byzantium, an initiative which received explicit papal sanction. The Greek population, depleted by Turkish razzias and Latin slavers, had apparently been paying tribute to the Turks, some of whom may have settled on the island while others served in its defense against the Hospital;[8] Turkish pirates from Rhodes had attacked Cyprus in 1303.[9] Rhodes was not easily taken, and early in 1307 the Hospital sent an embassy to Constantinople offering to hold the island from the emperor as his subjects, to defend it against the Turks, and also to provide him with 300 troops whenever he needed them. The emperor refused and even sent some galleys to help defend Rhodes, which held out and eventually surrendered on terms, probably in 1309.[10]

The Hospital's devious campaign was orchestrated with much cunning by the Master, the Provençal Fr. Foulques de Villaret, who at the end of 1306 left Cyprus for France where he persuaded the pope to finance a Hospitaller crusade. The leaders of the Order in the East envisaged the acquisition of Rhodes as a preliminary to the reconquest of the holy places; together with Cyprus, Rhodes would be used as a base for incursions along the Syrian coast and for the policing of a Latin blockade of Egypt. Villaret promised the recovery of Jerusalem or Antioch, but eventually in 1310 the considerable force of men and ships he succeeded in assembling sailed to the East and merely completed the Hospital's conquests on and around Rhodes. The Master induced certain neighboring Turks to attack the Emir of Menteshe, while the Hospital itself secured and temporarily held various castles on the mainland; its influence became so extensive that in 1311 some 250 merchants from Rhodes were said to be trading in the Emirate of Menteshe.[11] The Emir Masud proved unable to resist Hospitaller pressure. The Venetian Marino Sanudo Torsello wrote that he had spent much time on Rhodes with Villaret who "knew better than anyone in the world how to wage war and sow discord among the Turks and their neighbors," and who had reduced Masud "to nothing" by supporting other Turks such as Masud's son Orhkan and their kinsman *Strumbrachi*.[12]

Apart from conflicts among the Turks themselves, between Greek and Latin Christians, and between rival Latin powers and individuals, papal efforts to impose an economic blockade on western trade with the Muslims clashed with the interests of Latin merchants carrying war materials to Egypt and Syria from the West or moving slaves and other commodities southwards from the Black Sea and Aegean areas to Mamluk Egypt. At this time the papal prohibitions had been extended to cover all trade with Egypt, and they gave whoever captured any transgressors the right to retain their ships and goods and to ransom their persons. Fr. Foulques de Villaret not only attacked the Turks and occupied Karpathos and other islands claimed by the Venetians, but, in what could be justified as pursuit of papal policy, he also began in about 1311 to seize Genoese shipping which was contravening the papal trade prohibitions. Hospitaller galleys actually captured a Genoese galley returning from Alexandria as far west as the waters of Messina and took it to Rhodes. For the Italian commercial republics trade was vital; in retaliation, the Genoese seized Hospitaller ships and brethren and sold them in Turkey, and they bribed a large force of Turks from Menteshe to attack Rhodes and the 250 Rhodian merchants said to be on the mainland. Both Venice and Genoa began lengthy and ultimately successful lawsuits against the Hospital in order to repossess the Venetian islands and to secure reparations for Venetian and Genoese traders. The violent reaction of the major commercial powers to the most serious attempt to enforce the papal trade embargo was a decisive reverse in the economic war against the Mamluks. [13]

There was a general climate of hostility toward all the military orders, accompanied by demands for their union, reform or abolition. [14] These dissatisfactions were focused upon the Templars, but considerable hostility was also directed at the Hospital. Philip of France claimed in August 1312 that the pope had agreed to a thorough reform of that Order. [15] Both the French king and the prelates gathered at the Council of Vienne had strongly opposed the transfer of the Templars' lands to the Hospital, and their assent was secured only with great difficulty and on condition that the Hospital be reformed. The council meanwhile agreed on clauses which would have established that young and active Hospitallers should remain permanently overseas while the elderly administered the Order's western estates, that the Hospitallers' financial accounts should be audited by outsiders, that some of their privileges should be suspended, and that Hospitallers should be subject to the bishop of their diocese. The pope did, in fact, suspend their privileges, but, once the council was over, the whole reform program, potentially so damaging to the Hospital's activities, eventually lapsed. [16]

Foulques de Villaret's policies were undoubtedly astute. It cannot have been clear, even to contemporaries, precisely to what extent he had in 1306 forseen the assault on the Temple. Subsequently he was able to maneuver his Turkish allies and to manipulate the papal crusading machine to further the Hospital's conquests around Rhodes. The Master seems cleverly to have confused some potential opponents by spreading through western courts a variety of conflicting reports on events in the East and on his intentions there. There were brilliant initial successes. Between 1307 and 1312, while the Templars faced trial, torture, and dissolution, Villaret secured for the Hospital a military defensible base, gave it a politically justifiable function, and acquired for it the bulk of the Templars' lands. The papal bull suppressing the Temple was dated 22 March and made

public on 3 April 1312; a report of a Hospitaller victory
against a Turkish fleet, presumably against those Turks
from Menteshe who had been mobilized by the Genoese,
reached the pope with suspicious convenience on or just before 22 April; and just ten days later, on 2 May, the Templars' goods were transferred to the Hospital. Western reformers had called for a crusade, for a union of the military
orders, for military action against the infidel, and for the
enforcement of the papal embargo on Latin trade with the
Mamluks. In different ways Foulques de Villaret's policies
did something to satisfy each of these requirements, but
he proved too greedy, too overbearing, too financially extravagant, and in 1317 the Hospitallers on Rhodes deposed
him; one of the formal accusations against him was that he
had made an alliance with the Turks. [17]

In 1312 the Hospitallers attacked 23 Turkish ships passing Rhodes. The Turks fled to the island of Amorgos where
the Hospitallers burned their vessels and chased their crews
to the hilltops, slaughtering more than 800 Turks and let-
ting only ten or so escape, but the Turks had hurled rocks
down on their opponents, killing 57 Hospitallers and 300
of their men. [18] These were possibly the losses reported at
Avignon in April 1312 as amounting to 1500 Turks and 85
Latins. [19]

In 1318 and again in 1319 there were naval successes
against the Turks of Ephesus to the north of Menteshe. The
battle of 1318 was possibly that later described by Ludolf
of Sudheim in which the Hospitaller commander, Fr. Albert
von Schwarzburg, tricked the Turks, who came demanding
tribute. The Hospitallers killed men and women, young and
old, and took great booty, after which the Turks did not again
make demands for tribute. [20] The early-modern Cypriot chronicler Francesco Amadi mentioned that in 1318 two Hospitaller
galleys with two other vessels attacked and burned 32 Turkish
ships off Chios and killed or captured 3000 Turks; most of the
Turkish vessels must have been small ones. [21] In June 1319
some 24 ships with 80 Hospitallers and other mounted men
under Fr. Albert von Schwarzburg sailed from Rhodes to
Chios to join Martino Zaccaria, who had a galley and six
or so other ships; subsequently they met eleven Genoese galleys with whose help they defeated 29 Turkish vessels, ten

of them galleys, and 2600 men, killing or capturing more than 1500 Turks. Six Turkish vessels escaped, but other Turks who landed on Chios were killed or captured there. The Hospitallers then retook the island of Leros to the north of Rhodes where the Greeks had revolted, massacring the Hospitallers and their garrison, and appealing to Constantinople for help. Some of the Greeks, numbered at more than 1900, were killed and all the survivors were taken as captives to Rhodes. [22] The Florentine chronicler Giovanni Villani described a similar battle, which he dated to 1320, with 80 Turkish vessels facing four Hospitaller galleys and 20 smaller ships which were joined by six Genoese galleys returning from Cilicia; the galleys presumably overwhelmed lighter Turkish craft. The Turks attacked Rhodes but lost most of their fleet. They then fled to a nearby island where they had more than 5000 men waiting to invade Rhodes, and the Latins took them all: "they killed the old and sold the young as slaves." [23] A later version of Ludolf of Sudheim's text described how, at a date not given, the Hospitallers defeated 50 Turkish ships and chased their crews up a mountain on Kos where the Turks were able to kill many Christians. The Lord of Chios came to help the Hospitallers and tricked the Turks into allowing themselves to be taken to Rhodes, where all 6240 of them were massacred. [24] News of these events reached the West, or was later recorded there, with jumbled dates and numbers, but the pattern of Hospitaller victories in 1318, 1319, and possibly 1320 seems clear. [25]

One thread which ran through all these accounts was that of the wholesale slaughter of the enemy. Captured Turks were killed on numerous occasions, sometimes by crucifixion. However, the Hospitallers did have Turkish slaves as servants, though they were supposed to be careful in controlling their movements within the town at Rhodes. [26] The systematic execution of selected infidel captives was not a new tradition; for example, Saladin massacred his Templar and Hospitaller prisoners after the battle at Hattin in 1187. [27]

The Hospitallers had been notably effective in mobilizing a naval force in the Aegean, and their victories of 1306 to 1312 and of 1318 to 1319 or 1320 must have played some part in weakening Miletus and Ephesus as maritime centers, though both ports continued to export grain to Crete while Latin merchants still traded along the coast. [28] The focus of Turkish aggression on the Aegean shifted northwards to Smyrna where Umur of Aidin captured the castle by the sea from the Latins in 1329. The Hospitallers controlled Nissyros which they enfeoffed in 1316 to the Assanti family of Ischia, who were said to have secured it as ransom for a Turkish lord they had captured at sea. [29] Some time before 1319 the Hospital lost Kos, [30] which was not recovered until about 1336. [31] The Hospitallers had to fortify their islands, to settle Greek and Latin inhabitants, and to develop agriculture, commerce, and taxation so that men, money, ships, and supplies were available for the defense of Rhodes. [32] The Turkish mainland is clearly visible from the town of Rhodes which was easily attacked, yet the number of Hospitaller brethren in the East after 1306 was probably never higher than 250 or 300, although there were mercenary and militia forces. Most of these brethren were disciplined and experienced warriors whose military value was great, despite their limited numbers. The vast majority of the *fratres,* probably several thousand of them, were stationed in the commanderies of the West; many never fought against, or even saw, a Turk in their whole life. Their business, and it was an essential one, was to recruit and train brethren; to administer properties in order to produce a financial surplus to send to Rhodes; to sustain the spiritual life in the Order's communities in the West; and to maintain the image of Hospitaller achievement in the public eye.

* * *

At the time they invaded Rhodes the Hospitallers officially considered the island as a base ostensibly destined for operations which would lead to the recovery of Latin Syria, and subsequent hostilities against the Turks of Menteshe and Ephesus could still be presented as necessary for the maintenance of the sea-route to Cyprus and Syria. A decade later two different strands had become predominant in Latin policy. One amounted to a revival of the old confrontation with the schismatic Byzantine emperor who in 1329 recaptured Chios from Martino Zaccaria; in 1330 the pope could still write that Rhodes was threatened by the Greeks. [33] On the other hand, it was generally perceived that resistance to the Turks and the defense of the Latin East had become more important than the repetition of abortive schemes aimed at Jerusalem or Constantinople. In 1327 the Venetians were already attempting for the first time to draw both Byzantium and the Hospitallers into an anti-Turkish league.[34] In 1329 Umur of Aidin recaptured the castle by the sea at Smyrna from Martino Zaccaria, and in 1332 a Byzantine representative sailed to Rhodes and formally agreed to assist the Latins against the Turks. The pattern of alliances was, however, a fluctuating one. In 1333 the Master of the Hospital, in the light of quarrels between the Turkish emirates, suggested to the Venetians that they should make an alliance with Orhkan, Emir of Menteshe, and fight with him against other Turks, presumably Orhkan's enemies of Aidin who were in fact allied with the Greek emperor. This proposal for a revival of the policies of Fr. Foulques de Villaret came to nothing. Instead, probably in 1333 or early in 1334, the Hospital joined with other Latins in seizing the Byzantine island of Lesbos. Then, later in the year, the Hospitallers participated in decisive Latin victories both at sea and on land against Turks from Pergamon in Karasi, from Smyrna in Aidin, and from other parts; the Greeks, possibly because they were upset by the attack on Lesbos, did not join in this campaign.[35]

The confusion of alliances and objectives was illustrated by the Hospitallers' collaboration in the surprise attack on their Greek allies at Lesbos and their subsequent withdrawal from that enterprise. Probably in 1333 or 1334, and certainly before the naval action against the Turks of October 1334, the Hospitallers with four or five galleys joined the Genoese Domenico Cattaneo, Lord of Phokaia, and the Venetian Niccolò Sanudo, Duke of Naxos, in the conquest of Lesbos from Emperor Andronikos III. Nikephoros Gregoras claimed that the Latins were afraid the Greeks would attack them, but the occupation of Lesbos really marked a reversion to the tradition of opportunist Latin conquests of Byzantine islands; it may have occurred in the course of a patrol being operated by galleys of the Christian league. The Hospitallers seem to have withdrawn from the island quite soon, possibly in order to use their galleys against the Turks. Ac-

cording to Nikephoros Gregoras, the Hospitallers were tricked
by Domenico Cattaneo who seized the city for himself while
they were plundering the island, and so the Hospitallers departed in disgust, but John Kantakouzenos wrote that they
left in the face of an attack by the emperor because the
Hospital's men, quite possibly Rhodian Greeks, refused to
fight the emperor and because their commander would not
risk defeat and sailed back to Rhodes. Gregoras stated that
after October 1334 Andronikos mobilized powerful support
among his Turkish allies, after which Cattaneo called upon the
Hospitallers to mediate with the emperor, which they did,
witnessing the ensuing settlement. [36]

For two decades following the expensive conquest of
Rhodes and Villaret's extravagances the Hospital was paying off debts and absorbing the Templar's possessions. By
about 1335 the Order was financially solvent and building
up a credit with its Florentine bankers. In 1335 and 1336 the
Venetians and the Hospitallers prepared shipping and supplies for a further campaign which may have been directed
to the defense of the Christian kingdom in Cilician Armenia,
but the new pope, Benedict XII, stifled plans for a crusade,
and in 1337 the Venetians made treaties with Menteshe and
Aidin. The pope was faced with the outbreak of the Anglo-
French war and realized that if he proclaimed a crusade it
would be crippled by conflicts in the West and, furthermore,
that crusading tenths would be raised by the French king
and expended on the English war. Benedict must have been
reluctant to allow his own seriously threatened Florentine
banks, which were also the Hospital's bankers, to have the
Hospitallers' funds withdrawn; the result was not only inactivity along the Turkish coasts but also the loss to the
Hospital of a very considerable reserve, at least 360,000
florins, when the three great Florentine houses went bank-
rupt a few years later. [37] It was somewhat unfair for the next
pope, Clement VI, to accuse the Hospitallers in 1343 of inactivity and high living, and to threaten to take their possessions to create a new military order. [38]

In his bull which he may have exaggerated in order to
encourage the Hospitallers to mobilize for a new crusade,
Clement VI admitted that his judgments were based on
criticisms heard in the West. A different picture was drawn

by Ludolf of Sudheim who visited Rhodes at some time between 1336 and 1341. He described the flourishing and
impregnable base at Rhodes garrisoned by 350 *fratres* from
whom the Turks did not dare demand tribute; instead the
surrounding mainland paid a third of its produce as tribute
to Rhodes: *et totam circa terram et Turchiam pro tertia
parte proventuum habet sub tributo*. With other Turks,
presumably those beyond Menteshe further north in Aidin,
there was a truce on land but war both at sea and in certain
unnamed places from which damage was being inflicted
on the Christians. The Hospital still had a strong castle on
the mainland; the fertile island of Kos had been captured
and garrisoned; and the Hospitallers held the island of
Kastellorizo far to the south of Rhodes whence smoke and
mirror signals could be sent to give notice of Turkish activities, with the result that attacks on Christian shipping were
greatly reduced. [39] There was corruption in the western
priories, as Clement's bull of 1343 alleged. Truces in the
East, however advantageous and partial, could be represented at Avignon as inactivity. The Hospitallers were usually
able to muster three or four galleys, but their field of action
was limited by the papal discouragement of 1336, by the
virtual blocking of their funds, and by the Venetian treaties
of 1337. Quite possibly they had a truce with and received
tribute from Menteshe, while at some point well before 1348
they also made a commercial treaty with the ruler of Ephesus. [40] The major enemy now lay further north where Umur
of Aidin controlled Smyrna; in fact, the "Rhodians" were
among those being troubled by Umur in 1341. [41]

Umur's razzias provoked a reaction from Pope Clement
VI who insisted on a forceful Aegean policy. The Hospitallers participated fully in the Latin crusade which, in a surprise attack of October 1344, captured the sea-castle, though
not the citadel on the hill, at Smyrna which became a papal
city. The Hospitallers sent their galleys, provided a naval
base at Rhodes, and acted as papal paymaster for the crusading forces. Earlier, in May 1344, the Hospital had taken
part in a naval victory in which 52 Turkish ships were sunk.
After October Smyrna castle had to be held in difficult circumstances, with the Hospital playing a leading role in its
fortification and the Hospitaller Fr. Giovanni de Biandrate

being named captain-general of the papal fleet. [42] The following years were dramatically affected by the great plague, by a profound economic crisis, and by numerous European wars. To retain Smyrna was to deprive the Turks of a major naval base but also to reduce its commercial value, and for that Venetians and Genoese were reluctant to pay, especially after the Genoese had seized nearby Chios in June 1346. In that year, according to a contemporary Roman source, the Hospital prevented Venetian ships reaching Smyrna and even supplied arms and victuals to the Turks. [43] The Hospitallers were certainly quarrelling very seriously with the Venetians over various matters, [44] and they may also have made, probably in 1346, a one-year truce with Khizir, the Turkish ruler at Ephesus, and *ulu beg* or overlord of the Emirate of Aidin. [45] Though unreliable, the Roman chronicle was not uninformed, [46] and some kind of entente with some Turks must have been reached.

Hospitaller attitudes continued to fluctuate and ensuing events threw light on the religious or constitutional as well as the military and economic limitations and restrictions on policy. By 24 June 1347 news had reached Avignon that Hospitaller and other Latin galleys had taken 118 Turkish vessels, presumably mostly light ships, off Imbros and had captured their crews on the island; these Turks probably came from Aidin and the neighboring emirates. Yet in April 1347, before this naval success, the Master at Rhodes forbade the captain of the Hospitaller galleys to assume any responsibility for the defense of Smyrna; by then the Master must have known that on 28 November 1346 Clement VI and his cardinals had sanctioned secret negotiations for a ten-year truce there. The pope himself felt the constraints of Latin opinion. On 5 February 1348 Clement VI wrote to his legates who were negotiating with Umur of Smyrna and to his brother Khizir of Ephesus whose terms involved the demolition of the sea-castle at Smyrna. Given the multiple crises in the West, Clement agreed to a truce which would allow the Turks a half of the *commerclum* or port duties at Smyrna, but he could not sanction the demolition of a castle which had been captured by a crusade since that would provoke the disapproval of Christendom.

The situation changed in April 1348 when the great Umur

was killed, and a few months later Khizir agreed to proposals presented by the Hospitaller Fr. Dragonet de Joyeuse and sent envoys to Avignon to secure papal ratification of them. Khizir was prepared to make considerable concessions and to accept Christian trade, consuls, churches, and bishops within his territories; to grant the Latins half the *commerclum* of Ephesus and other cities; to disarm his own fleet; and to confirm an earlier pact, possibly a commercial one, made with the Hospital. Though this truce had been negotiated by a Hospitaller, he was acting in the pope's name and any agreement was subject to papal approval. The text took the unilateral form common to Muslim pacts with Latins; dated 18 August 1348, it was a document of Khizir in which he made various promises while the other parties, the Latins, neither promised nor subscribed. Though never ratified by the pope, partly owing to opposition from the Venetians who wanted to revive the Latin league, the truce was presumably applied for a while since the text laid down that it was to be considered as valid until Khizir's envoys should return from Avignon. The proposals were drawn up in Greek and Latin by a Greek notary of the Hospital, Georgios Kalokires, and were signed by Khizir who swore on the Koran to respect them. [47] This did amount to negotiations with the infidel and would in fact have secured the Latins a very considerable income from Ephesus and the cities, but the Hospital could never make the elaborate permanent arrangements for the payment of tribute to the Turks and the protection of its islands which the Venetians of Crete periodically reached with the emirates.

The Hospital, although it had to pay 3000 florins a year for the defense of Smyrna, was not expected to defend the castle single-handed. The brethren and their small fleet took part in a succession of further crusading expeditions, notably at Alexandria in 1365, at Nikopolis in 1396, and on other lesser occasions. It did so as a matter of routine and duty rather than enthusiasm, though the brethren usually fought with professional courage and competence when the occasion arose. The Hospitallers had become a military machine whose existence tended to become an end in itself; the cheapest and safest policy was that of staying on their islands behind stone fortifications and avoiding conflict, even when

successive popes denounced their inertia and threatened
to confiscate their western possessions or to transfer their
seat to the mainland, presumably to Smyrna. [48] Most of
the brethren were ordinary people with no special vocation
who seldom expressed their feelings on paper. Many of them
came from the lesser gentry or urban bourgeoisie and were
men with little formal education whose motives are difficult
to gauge. They seem never to have learnt Turkish, and it
is uncertain how much they knew about Islam or about
Muslim culture. Philippe de Mézières, who had spent years
in the East and understood the situation well, alleged that
the Hospitallers had fallen into decline and only went to
serve at Rhodes in order to secure a rich commandery in
the West. [49] There must have been an element of truth in
this, but many Hospitallers did pass much of their career
in the East, and it was also true that a period of service at
Rhodes followed by an administrative position in the West
formed a regular part of their pattern of service.

* * *

From 1306 to 1348 the Hospitallers were established
once more in an area where they confronted an infidel enemy,
conquering Rhodes and various surrounding islands, defeat-
ing the fleets of Menteshe and Ephesus, and assisting in the
capture and defense of Smyrna. The Emirates of Aiden
and Menteshe continued for another forty years to raid the
Morea and the Aegean islands and to attack Latin shipping, [50] but their naval power was at least partially contained. Predominance among the Turkish emirates and the
center of attraction for the *ghazi* and warrior elements in
Anatolian society shifted northwards once again to the predominantly land-based Ottoman forces which moved permanently into Europe; the Ottomans occupied Gallipoli in
the Dardanelles in 1354, and by 1402 they controlled a large
part of the Balkans. In 1359 some fifty Hospitallers formed
part of a force which attacked a Turkish tower at Lampsakos
in the Dardanelles, courageously covering the Latins' retreat when the Turks counter-attacked in force. [51] Thereafter, for the next fifteen years or more, the Hospital had
little contact with the Ottoman Turks who lacked an effective
fleet.

From 1361, when they sent four galleys to Adalia and covered the retreat of the Cypriot forces there, [52] the Hospitallers were implicated in Cypriot assaults on coastal towns in southern Anatolia, Syria, and Egypt. When Pierre de Lusignan, King of Cyprus, assembled a great fleet at Rhodes in 1365, the Emirs of Ephesus and Miletus hastened in their fear to offer him tribute, presents, and provisions, and the king made a written peace with them at the Hospitallers' request. The Hospital provided four galleys and 100 brethren for this crusade which briefly captured Alexandria, and it furnished four galleys and twelve light craft for attacks on Tripoli and Adalia in 1367. [53] After the crusade of 1365 sacked Alexandria, the Egyptians threatened a counter-attack and called on the Anatolian emirates to collaborate, which caused the Hospitallers to summon 100 brethren to Rhodes on 1 March 1366. [54] Certain indignant emirs had already prohibited the customary export of horses and foodstuffs to Rhodes. [55] Such imports were necessary to the Hospitallers who secured papal licenses to bring in grain and other supplies from the mainland with the usual restrictions on supplying infidels with iron, wood, or other war materials. [56] These imports did in fact continue, [57] and a commercial treaty with Miletus was made some time before 1391 and was renewed soon after August 1402. [58]

The Hospital was increasingly crippled by the general economic and demographic catastrophe in the West which seriously reduced its incomes and military manpower. [59] Yet as the Ottomans continued their advances into the Balkans, Pope Gregory XI turned to the Hospitallers as his only hope of effective military action, even on a minor scale. In 1374 Gregory made the Hospital entirely responsible for the defense of Smyrna, and there was a project for the Order to occupy and defend two Byzantine towns, Thessalonika and, quite probably, Gallipoli which had been retaken in 1366. That scheme came to nothing, but the pope continued to press for an expedition to the East; in 1377 the Hospital occupied the Latin part of the Morea or Peloponnesos which it had leased for five years, and in 1378 the Hospitallers invaded Epiros in northern Greece where they were decisively defeated by the Christian Albanian ruler of Arta, apparently without making any direct contact with the Turks.

This defeat was partly caused by the death of Gregory XI in March 1378 and the election of Urban VI who failed to send reinforcements to Greece, but it was also true that for decades the papacy had favored its wars in Italy at the expense of the Latin East. During Gregory's pontificate the most the Hospital could expect from him was 3000 florins a year for the defense of Smyrna, while the pope was spending an annual average of well over 194,000 florins on his Italian wars. [60]

There was still little or no direct confrontation between the Hospital and the Ottomans. In 1378 the Latin West was divided by a papal schism which was, until about 1409, reflected by a split within the Hospital which further reduced the manpower and money reaching Rhodes. Thus the Priory of Catalunya complained that only nine out of twenty-one western priories were sending any dues, and that neither pope was contributing to the defense of Smyrna, "the key to Turkey": *la Ciutat de la Esmira la qual es clau de la Turquia.* [61] From 1382 to 1396 and from 1409 to 1420 the Master was absent from Rhodes dealing with these interrelated political and financial problems in the West. [62] On 20 March 1389 the walls of Smyrna were badly damaged by an earthquake and needed to be rebuilt, [63] and in the same year a new Ottoman leader, Bayezid, initiated large-scale conquests in Anatolia, rapidly occupying Aiden and Menteshe, blockading and besieging Smyrna, and prohibiting the export of grain and other supplies from the mainland to Rhodes. [64] While the Venetians sought new treaties with Bayezid, the Hospital decided to raise heavier taxes in the West. In 1390 it arranged to send a contingent of brethren to Rhodes. [65] In that year the Avignonese pope, Clement VII, granted a general indulgence which by 1392 had produced more than 25,000 florins for the refortification of Smyrna, a considerable sum compared with the Hospital's average annual western income of 38,500 florins available for transfer to Rhodes from the West. [66] It was agreed at Avignon in July 1392 to restrict the perimeter of the *ciuitas* at Smyrna so that it could be defended more effectively and less expensively. [67]

These difficulties were compounded in 1393 when the Hospitallers refused a proposal from Bayezid for a peace on both land and sea because they were unable to accept that all slaves who escaped either to Smyrna or to Rhodes should be returned to the Turks, or that Bayezid's subjects should be able to trade freely at Rhodes and to sell slaves there. [68] The issue of baptized slaves represented a point of principle on which a Christian religious order could not compromise; the projected truce with Khizir of 1348 had included a clause enjoining the return of slaves by all parties, but it left each party with the alternative of making a payment instead. [69] In 1394 the Hospitallers' island of Astypalia had been so devastated by certain Turks that it was no longer inhabited; in 1395 Turks were feared to be cruising in the islands north of Rhodes while the men of Kastellorizo far to the south were then in truce with the Turks on the mainland nearby. [70] In mid-1394, however, the situation was partly saved when the Hospitaller captain at Smyrna captured two or more sons of a leading Turkish official, the *subashi* of Smyrna, and in return for their release secured a seven-year truce with the Turks of Smyrna who had to pay 10,000 gold ducats as a pledge that they would observe it. [71] There seems to have been no further threat to Smyrna until 1402.

A much more serious danger was that the Ottomans would dominate the whole of the Balkans and capture Constantinople, which Bayezid began to besiege in 1394. In 1396 a major relief force of Latin and Hungarian crusaders was decisively crushed by Bayezid and his Christian Serbian vassals at Nikopolis on the Danube. The fault lay with the Westerners and their lack of tactical restraint; however, Fr. Philibert de Naillac, Master-elect of the Hospital, did not join the French forces in their rash advance but stayed in the rear with Sigismund of Hungary and helped him to escape down the Danube. [72] The Nikopolis campaign may, nonetheless, have saved Constantinople. It forced Bayezid to raise the siege and it destroyed a considerable part of his army; Sigismund, who had to return by sailing down the Danube and taking a route through the Mediterranean, wrote to Naillac in November 1396 that he had reached Constantinople just in time to prevent its fall to the Turks; [73] and the French Marshal Boucicault, who had been captured at Nikopolis, took decisive aid to the Byzantine capital in the following years, assisted by two Hospitaller galleys which during 1399 participated by land and sea in attacks on the Turks in and around the Bosphorus. The Hospitallers helped to raise large sums of money to ransom various noble Frenchmen some of whom, including Jean de Nevers, son of the Duke of Burgundy, visited Rhodes on their way home from captivity in Anatolia. [74] This must have raised the Hospital's prestige in western courts, and Burgundian help was to do much to save Rhodes in the sieges it underwent between 1440 and 1444. [75]

The Hospitallers opposed the Turks elsewhere, notably in Greece. Just as between 1334 and 1347 they had joined Latin leagues designed to contain Turkish aggression at sea in the Aegean, so from 1388 to 1402 they again initiated, negotiated for, and participated in Latin naval unions against the Turks. [76] In 1390 they sent two galleys and a number of brethren who helped the Emperor Manuel II, who had fled to Rhodes, to recover Constantinople from his nephew John VII. The Russian traveller Ignatius of Smolensk remarked on these Hospitallers as the "Romans whose emblem was a white cross sewn on their chests; they contended bravely with their enemies." The Hospitallers may have felt that they were justified in attacking the Christian John VII because he was in open alliance with Turkish troops. [77] After Nikopolis, the Hospitallers returned to their earlier Greek schemes. From 1356 onwards there was apparently an element of opinion which favored establishing the Hospital in mainland Greece, ostensibly in order to defend it against the Turks, but also in the hope of enlarging the Hospital's domains and incomes while placing themselves in a more central position from which to resist the Turks. Even after the unsuccessful leasing of the Latin Morea in 1377 and their miserably abortive invasion of Epirus in 1378, the Hospitallers made further efforts to acquire claims in the Latin Morea between about 1384 and 1389. In 1397 they occupied the great castle at Corinth, doing much to save the Peloponnesos from Turkish invasion or occupation, and by 1400 they had purchased the whole of the Byzantine Despotate of the Morea comprising the southeastern part of the Peloponnesos.

According to Manuel II, only the Hospitallers had the strength and enthusiasm to defend the Peloponnesos, and

they were anxious to acquire the whole peninsula, hoping
to mobilize support for their action in the West. Manuel
was, after all, a Greek and somewhat ambiguous about the
Latin Hospitallers, but he characterized them as well dis-
posed, trustworthy, and famed for their opposition to the
Turks, correctly describing them as vowed to chastity, obedience, poverty, and the fight against the infidel. Manuel,
who had travelled in the West, wrote:

> Let no one assume by looking at their few galleys
> stationed in Rhodes that the strength of the Hos-
> pitallers is weak and feeble. When they wish to
> do so a great number of them can assemble from
> all over the world where they are scattered. They
> are men for whom nothing is more important than
> what is conducive to good courage, warfare and
> a noble spirit. To them it is far better to die with
> glory than to offer their enemies the opportunity
> of exulting and inflicting wounds on the backs of
> men who are in retreat.

The Greek populace rose against this Latin occupation,
but, as Manuel said, "The Turks were more apprehensive
of the Hospitallers than of any other power." Their presence
in the Peloponnesos was so effective that eventually, late
in 1401 or early in 1402, Bayezid offered the despot Theodore peace on the sole condition that the Hospital should
withdraw. [78]

Then, in July 1402, the overall balance of forces was
completely altered when the Mongol ruler Timur defeated
Bayezid near Ankara. Constantinople was saved once again;
many of the Aegean coastal dynasties dispossessed by Bayezid
were restored to their emirates; and the Hospital renewed
its old commercial treaty with the Emir of Miletus which
must have dated back before 1391, so that by April 1403
merchants were trading at Miletus. [79] Smyrna posed an
awkward dilemma but, after some debate, the Hospitallers
at Rhodes decided that its defense should take precedence
over their interests in Greece; measures to strengthen Smyrna
against the Ottomans had, in fact, been taken well before
their defeat in July 1402. [80] In September two Hospitaller
galleys sailed to the island of Samos to encourage those Turks

who had fled there with their shipping to continue their resistance to Timur, who was advancing westwards, and to prevent him securing their vessels. [81] The Genoese of Chios and Phokaia formally submitted and paid tribute to Timur, [82] but the Hospital was constitutionally bound to reject such demands from an infidel; in that instance religious considerations were crucial. After fierce resistance, Smyrna was destroyed and dismantled in one of the great Timur's few victories over Latin Christians, one for which he had a special religious motive in that he wished to be seen as a *ghazi* leader victorious against a non-Muslim enemy. [83] The chroniclers on all sides recounted the details of an epic two-week siege, but some contemporaries suggested that after a spirited defense the Captain of Smyrna, Fr. Iñigo de Alfaro, and the Hospitaller garrison may have agreed to sail away, leaving more than a thousand Greek Christian refugees to be slaughtered by Timur who then destroyed much of the town and its fortress. [84] It was claimed that it would cost more than 100,000 florins to rebuild the castle. [85] Timur soon moved away from western Anatolia having temporarily destroyed Ottoman predominance there and leaving the Hospital to face the coastal emirates as it had done before 1391. In September 1403 the Castilian Ruy Gonçalez de Clavijo noted a garrison of 100 men at Kos while the Hospital also held Kalymnos and Leros, the latter having been attacked by Turks from Miletus in the same year. [86]

Bayezid died in captivity while his sons scattered in different directions and fought each other, yet the Greeks and Latins did not turn on the Ottomans whose position in Europe remained largely intact. The Christian powers were afraid of Timur, and as late as April 1403 the Hospitallers had spies reporting on Timur's movements which still perturbed them. [87] In about January 1403, the Greeks and Latins made an alliance with Suleyman who had taken his father Bayezid's place in Ottoman Europe. This pact provided for combined Christian-Ottoman operations in the event of an invasion of Europe by Timur, though it also restricted the movements of the Ottoman fleet and involved the surrender by Suleyman of extensive territories and tributes. By the treaty the Hospital was to receive the town of Salona north of Athens which it seems not in the end to have occupied. [88] This pact showed that the Hospital could be party to extensive arrangements with Muslims. In fact, in the same year, 1403, the Hospitallers negotiated an elaborate treaty with the Mamluk Sultan, who eventually failed to ratify it, which would have assured the Hospital virtual control of the lucrative pilgrim traffic to Jerusalem. [89] In June 1403 various Turks and their Latin vassal Antonio Acciaiuoli attacked the Hospitallers at Corinth, [90] but on the whole the major threat to Christian Greece had been averted by the defeat of Bayezid, and during 1404 the Hospitallers withdrew from the mainland, having helped to prevent the Ottomans from occupying the Morea during the crucial years between Nikopolis in 1396 and Ankara in 1402. [91]

In mid-1403 the Hospitallers participated in the Marshal Boucicault's ill-judged and inconclusive razzias on the coasts of southern Anatolia and Syria for which Rhodes was the principal base; the Hospital could scarcely refuse to collaborate in these sporadic attacks on the infidel which were initiated by the French and Genoese. [92] The Hospital no longer had a function in Greece, and, partly as a result of the schism, it was seriously short of money. After losing Smyrna, the Hospitallers needed to establish a new Turkish front to parade in the West and they were tempted to play upon Turkish rivalries which were extremely complex. In mid-1405 the Hospital proposed to fortify Tenedos at the mouth of the Dardanelles, but that suggestion was rejected by the Venetians. [93] Then, in about 1407, the upstart Junayd, who came from the Smyrna region and had secured support from Suleyman in Europe, ousted the rulers of Aidin whom Timur had restored; they in their turn summoned help from Suleyman's rival and brother Mehmet who ruled in the northeastern part of Anatolia. Suleyman made plans to sail to Smyrna and rebuild the walls formerly defended there by the Hospitallers but destroyed by Timur, whereupon the Master Fr. Philibert de Naillac went to Smyrna with three galleys and offered to assist Mehmet against Suleyman. Once there, Naillac began to construct a great tower at his own expense, evidently hoping to re-establish control of the port before any of the Turkish rulers could do so. Mehmet pulled down this unfinished work, upon which event Naillac is said to have threatened that the pope would

send a great army to destroy Mehmet. The latter replied
that the Hospitallers were the implacable enemies of the
Turks on land and at sea, and that the destruction of Latin
Smyrna was Timur's one good deed since the castle had
permitted many Christian slaves to escape from Turkish lands:

> "Nonetheless, let us do as you wish but without
> annoying the Turks. I offer you as much land as
> you require on the borders of Caria and Lycia. Go
> and build whatever kind of fortress you desire."
> After giving careful consideration to these words,
> the Grand Master replied to Mehmet, "Ruler, give
> me instead a portion of the lands under your do-
> minion and do not send me to foreign provinces."
> Mehmet replied, "But I am giving you what is mine
> since I have awarded the province to Menteshe.
> Have no further concern." Requesting first a writ-
> ten decree, which he received, the Grand Master
> then departed. [94]

Contrary to his protestations, Mehmet was in effect buy-
ing the Hospital out of Smyrna by granting it something
outside the region he controlled. There at Bodrum in 1407
or 1408 the Hospitallers built a castle, despite opposition
from Emir Ilyas of Menteshe who arrived with a force to
prevent them. [95] There seems to have been at least some
fighting while the Hospitallers were building their fortress
there. [96]

The castle at Bodrum was undoubtedly a replacement
for that at Smyrna, and both had the same dedication to
St. Peter. Its construction was in part a fund-raising exercise which enabled the Hospital to claim that it had a foot-
hold in Asia which was in direct contact with the infidel and
was an annoyance to the Turks since it offered an escape
route for Christian slaves, as indeed it did. [97] Bodrum, however, was scarcely an outpost of strategic importance. [98] It
was situated on a barren peninsula, difficult of access by
land and calculated to give minimum irritation to the Turks,
while the Hospitallers already controlled the channel between
Kos and the mainland from their castle on Kos. Furthermore, the castle at Bodrum stood out to sea on an isthmus
which was strongly defended across a narrow strip of land

and was easily provisioned from nearby Kos. The Hospitallers knew well how to profit from their investment. In October 1408 a group of French Hospitallers sailed to defend the castle, and on 3 December 1408 the French king granted the Hospitallers a tax exemption in view of their losses at Bodrum and the advantages there for escaping Christian slaves. The number of Christians and others who escaped may have been rather small, but the possibility clearly irritated the Turks and provided the Hospital with a propaganda point which inspired religiously motivated responses in the West. In a later exemption of 1414 the French king spoke of the expenditure at Bodrum of more than 100,000 francs, and a further royal privilege was granted in 1416. The English gave financial help, and in 1418 the king's uncle, the Bishop of Winchester, sent beams and planks for the work at Bodrum. The papacy also contributed. On 30 July 1409 the Master Fr. Philibert de Naillac, who was at the Council of Pisa helping to settle the papal schism, secured from the new pope, Alexander V, a five-year indulgence which was to support the defense of Bodrum and which referred to the expense and loss of men there: *non sine magna strage et effusione sanguinis hominum in dicta terra Turcorum.* This indulgence was confirmed on 30 August 1412 by Alexander V's successor, John XXIII, who spoke of expenditures at Bodrum of up to 70,000 florins. [99]

It evidently suited the Hospitallers to emphasize, and presumably to exaggerate, their expenses and losses when seeking privileges from benefactors in the West. The reality of the situation was reflected in instructions issued at Rhodes on 14 December 1409 ordering the captain at Bodrum to avoid skirmishes or *scaramuce* with the Turks lest they provoke serious Turkish retaliations. [100] To some extent the Hospital's ideological struggle against the infidel was confused with a hunt for booty on the part of individual brethren. Thus the authorities on Chios complained that a *galiotta* armed by the garrison at Bodrum had seized and robbed shipping from Chios; on 18 January 1412 the government at Rhodes hastened to excuse the Hospital, to return the captured merchandise, and to explain that Bodrum castle had been built not to rob Christians but to combat the enemies of the faith. [101] At the same time individual Hospi-

tallers were arming quasi-private raiding vessels to attack
infidel shipping and sharing the eventual booty in proportion to the original investments of the partners. Two French
Hospitallers received a license at Rhodes on 14 April 1413
permitting them to use their *galiotta* to attack infidels who
were the enemies of the Hospital and any subjects of such
infidels, excepting the Orthodox monks of Mount Athos or
their goods; yet by 5 August of that same year there was a
complaint from a *burgensis* of Rhodes that his ship and his
goods had been taken near Cyprus by those very Frenchmen
who had just been licensed for the *corso*. [102]

The Ottomans gradually re-established their predominance in Anatolia, but for a while the old coastal emirates
confronted the Hospitallers. The ships of Emir Ilyas of
Menteshe continued to make sorties from Miletus. In 1411
the Hospitallers and a certain Viscount *dacy* made an attack
on Makri, the modern Fetiye on the coast of the southern
part of Menteshe. Fr. Raymond de Lescure, Prior of Toulouse,
was killed there. At the end of 1411 the Hospital was at peace
with the Turks of Ephesus, but unidentified Turks, probably
from Menteshe, attacked Syme and other Hospitaller islands;
and these or other Turks were threatening Bodrum castle
by January 1412 when the guard-galley from Rhodes was
being sent to protect the castle and the islands. With the
Ottomans who were based on Gallipoli there was peace on land
and within the Dardanelles, but the Hospitallers felt at lib-
erty to attack them at sea elsewhere, as they explained to
Jacopo Gattilusio, Lord of Lesbos, who in the spring of 1412
seized and tortured the crew of a Hospitaller ship which had
captured a Turkish *galiotta* and unloaded its cargo on Lesbos.
Jacopo Gattilusio presumably feared Ottoman reprisals,
but the Hospitallers maintained that their galleys could jus-
tifiably attack Ottoman shipping outside the Dardanelles:
*cum notorium sit quod galee nostre armate quando reperi-
untur in marj extra strictum Romanie cum aliquibus lignis
turchorum armatis iuste posse capere et lucrarj.*

In Ottoman Europe Suleyman was replaced by his brother
Musa in 1411. In February 1413 there were fears at Rhodes
that Musa would attack with the Ottoman fleet based at
Gallipoli, and the Hospitallers suggested the reconstitution
of the former anti-Turkish Latin league to resist Musa. Then

in July 1413 Musa was killed and another brother Mehmet, with whom the Hospital had been friendly in about 1407, became the sole Ottoman ruler. A period of uneasy equilibrium followed at sea as Mehmet began to subdue the Anatolian coastal emirates. In or just before April 1415 the government at Rhodes instructed the captain of a Hospitaller galley then at Chios to reply evasively to a demand from Mehmet for two Hospitaller galleys to give assistance against Junayd of Ephesus and against Mehmet's other Turkish enemies, who may have included Ilyas of Menteshe. The captain was to answer that the Hospital was at peace with the Turks on land and that he was guarding the seas to prevent the escape of Mehmet's enemies. However, a document dated at Rhodes on 25 April 1415 declared that Mehmet had subdued all the Turks except those of Menteshe and that the Hospital was at peace with Mehmet and all other infidels, including presumably those of Menteshe. Mehmet may well have reduced Junayd, who had usurped control in the Smyrna region, to tributary status at this time. Subsequently there were apparently a few years with no major conflict between Hospitallers and Turks. The period in which the Hospital was able to play the Turks off against one another came to an end soon after 1421, in which year the Master Naillac, the Sultan Mehmet, and the Emir Ilyas all died. [103]

The situation was full of contradictions. Sometime before 1410 there was a Hospitaller mission to the Emir of Karaman. Then in 1412 the Hospitallers appointed a *burgensis* of Rhodes as consul at Adalia for the whole Emirate of Karaman in the south-central part of Anatolia. They replaced him with another Rhodian *burgensis* in 1413 and yet another in 1414.[104] However, trade was in some ways restricted, and an edict of 1414 prohibited the carrying of certain goods, presumably war materials, to the infidel.[105] In 1412 the Hospital was at peace with Ephesus but feared an attack on Bodrum from Miletus, while it was prepared to attack Ottoman shipping outside the Dardanelles. In 1415 the Hospital was at peace with the "Turks" by land but not at sea. The Latins of Lesbos and Chios were more vulnerable and more careful to avoid offense than those of Rhodes, but the Hospitallers had their truces and alliances with the

Muslims, seeking to balance and oppose the various rival
emirs. After 1421 this was to become increasingly difficult.
In May 1422 two Turkish ships off Marmaris were threatening the island of Rhodes. The Hospital's enemies at Adalia
and Alanya had six large vessels and had recently burnt
the ship of a Rhodian *burgensis*; and the Hospitallers were
alarmed that their enemy Junayd, who had taken Ephesus
and other *seignories*, was arming a large fleet. [106]

* * *

The Hospital conducted a strictly limited operation. A
small, efficiently organized and well-commanded elite could
achieve results out of all proportion to their number. The
Hospital's standing navy and army were minimal, but it was
also the case that the few hundred Hospitallers serving in
the East were supported by several thousand brethren and
large numbers of tenants and serfs in the West. Brethren
were sometimes discouraged from travelling to Rhodes or
were even sent back to the West in order to avoid expense.
Local forces could be raised and there was a small group of
Rhodian subjects with a continuous military tradition; thus
a certain Niquita de Assiza claimed in 1400 that his Syrian
ancestors had taken part in the conquest of Rhodes, that
his uncle Soloman from Jerusalem had died serving the Hospital at Imbros, and that two other uncles had been killed
in the Order's service, one at Smyrna and one on Kos. [107] Con-
taining the Turks at sea from a well-defended offshore island
involved very different policies from those of the Teutonic
Order which campaigned regularly across vast territories
and even assisted western knights to raise the funds which
enabled so many of them to travel to fight in Prussia. [108] When
the future Henry IV of England visited Rhodes while on
pilgrimage in 1392, he and his companions had their arms
painted on wooden shields to display in the Master's palace,
probably in imitation of the similar practice in Prussia, [109] and
a row of stone shields, paid for by the English king and a
group of his nobles, later decorated the tower at Bodrum. [110]
Yet there was no stream of chivalric Westerners travelling to
Rhodes or Bodrum, nor was there any regular military
confrontation with the Turks which would have attracted
them to do so.

The Hospital's conflicts with the Latin mercantile republics and with the schismatic Christians of Byzantium were carefully kept under control, and those powers normally had sound reasons for discouraging the Hospitallers from precipitating any major conflict with the Turks. The Hospital had to avoid extremes. Latin war fleets normally defeated Turkish navies, but to maintain galleys at sea for any length of time was exorbitantly costly, as was the permanent defense of any mainland bridgehead. The Hospitallers were little concerned with the Turks' internal affairs, and had no serious thought of conquests in Anatolia or of the abolition of Latin trade there. They aimed to defend Rhodes and to provide a measure of security on the Aegean. The Latins did not seek a lucrative luxury trade in the emirates but needed grain and other products to sustain their island populations. The Turks wanted booty and tribute, but were also anxious for commerce and the customs dues paid on it. Open hostilities were often followed by truces and commercial pacts.

The Hospital at Rhodes confronted no serious opposition from local bishops or from hostile nobles and estates, and it suffered no major defeat to compare with the battle at Tannenberg in 1410 when the power of the Teutonic Order was shattered by the Christian Poles. The Hospitallers composed the schism within their own order in 1409, and they escaped unscathed from the extended discussion at the Council of Constance between 1415 and 1418 when the whole question of the canonical purposes and powers of a military order was bitterly debated with much publicity by the representatives of the Polish king and of the Teutonic Order.[111] The Hospital had to overcome such enormous difficulties that its very survival was an outstanding achievement. It preserved its existence as an institution without degenerating into a self-perpetuating corporation defending only itself. Rhodes became an important naval and commercial base in the Aegean and on the sea route to Cyprus, Syria, and Egypt, and its defense contributed considerably to Latin resistance in the Levant. The Hospitallers did face fundamental ambiguities: the religious frontier was often vague since there were dissenting minorities on either side of it, while Christians almost inevitably traded with Turks, hired them as mercernaries, served them as vassals, paid them tribute, and concluded alliances or ententes with them.

The brethren may naturally have viewed the Hospital as providing them a career, but they knew also that they were Latin Christians and members of a religious order which had been established on Rhodes in order to oppose the Turks. In 1412 the Hospitallers in the Convent were so exasperated by Pope John XXIII's sale of the nomination to the Commandery of Cyprus to King Janus's five-year-old illegitimate son and by other papal provisions to priories and commanderies, that they threatened, with some effect, to leave Rhodes unless the pope renounced such damaging interferences. Exactly a hundred years after Clement V suppressed the Temple and the Hospitallers' lands had been in danger from those who accused them of inaction, the brethren at Rhodes wrote bitterly to the pope:

> Our patrimony is constituted through benefactions made by the faithful with the intention of creating resources for our works of hospitality and for the expeditions which we conduct against the infidels; is it not a contradiction of the Order's statutes and of the donors' intentions to employ this patrimony to remunerate the services of courtiers and to prevent the Convent and the Grand Master from using it to recompense blood which has been shed in favor of the Christian cause? [112]

The various Spanish and German military orders gradually lost their *raison d'être* as, at different stages, their infidel opponents were overrun or converted to Christianity, [113] but the Hospitallers were actively defending part of a frontier in continual contraction so that, as the Turks continued their advances and Rhodes became more isolated, the island's defense became increasingly important. In this sense, the Hospital came to depend on the Turks for its existence and incomes. The Order was, however, restricted by certain limitations of an essentially religious character; it could make temporary truces or pacts and commercial agreements with the infidel, but it could not pay them tribute or hand over baptized Christians to them. In 1454, following the fall of Constantinople, when the Sultan demanded submission and threatened to destroy Rhodes, the Master is said to have replied to the Ottoman envoys:

This island does not belong to me. As you are subject to your own lord, I also am subject to the pope. The pope has commanded me to pay tribute to no one. It is not only to your ruler, who belongs to an alien nation and is a believer in an alien faith, that I am forbidden to pay tribute but I may not even do so to any of the kings of our compatriots and co-religionists.[114]

Notes

*The author is most grateful to Elizabeth Zachariadou for advice on a number of points and to the Institute for Advanced Study at Princeton where this work was prepared.

1. The sources for the history of Menteshe and Aidin are woefully scarce; the standard works are P. Wittek, *Das Fürstentum Mentesche: Studie zur Geschichte Westkleinasiens im 13.-15. Jh.* (Istanbul, 1934), and E. Zachariadou, *Trade and Crusade: Venetian Crete and the Emirates of Menteshe and Aydin (1300-1415)* (Venice, 1983); in the case of the Ottomans, P. Lindner, *Nomads and Ottomans in Medieval Anatolia* (Bloomington, 1983), pp. 1-50, provides weighty arguments for revising, or even rejecting, Wittek's "*ghazi* thesis." H. Inalcik, "The Rise of the Turcoman Maritime Principalities in Anatolia," *Byzantinische Forschungen*, IX (1986), appeared after this paper was completed.

2. H. Gibb (trans.), *The Travels of Ibn Battuta: AD 1325-1354*, 2 vols. (Cambridge, 1958-1962), II, 427-453 (dated at pp. 528-532).

3. *Ibid.*, II, 446-447.

4. Cited in Lindner, *Nomads and Ottomans...*, p. 3.

5. The standard work is J. Delaville le Roulx, *Les Hospitaliers à Rhodes jusqu'à la mort de Philibert de Naillac: 1310-1421* (Paris, 1913), with additional materials in A. Luttrell, *The Hospitallers in Cyprus, Rhodes, Greece and the West: 1291-1440* (London, 1978), and *idem, Latin Greece, the Hospitallers and the Crusade: 1291-1440* (London, 1982). For the period 1391-1421, *idem, The Later History of the Maussolleion and its Utilization in the Hospitaller Castle at Bodrum* ("Jutland Archaeological Society Publications," XV, part 2 /Copenhagen, 1986/), and *idem, Notes and Documents on the Aftermath of the Battle at Ankara: 1402-1403* /provisional title: forthcoming/; for the general background, see K. Setton, *The Papacy and the Levant: 1204-1571*, 2 vols. (Philadelphia, 1976-1978). N. Housley, *The Avignon Papacy and the Crusades: 1305-1378* (Oxford, 1986), contains important materials but appeared after this paper had been completed. See also A. Luttrell, "Papauté et Hôpital: l'Enquête de 1373," in A.-M. Legras (ed.), *l'Enquête*

pontificale de 1373 sur l'Ordre des Hospitaliers de Saint-Jean de Jérusalem, I (Paris, 1987).

6. These points are briefly discussed in A. Luttrell, "Templari e Ospitalieri in Italia," in M. Roncetti *et al.* (eds.), *Templari e Ospitalieri in Italia: la Chiesa di San Bevignate a Perugia* (Perugia, 1987). The military orders varied greatly, and some contemporaries, such as Jacques de Vitry, held that their aims did include the fight against schismatics and heretics: J. Riley-Smith, *What Were the Crusades?* (London, 1977), pp. 70-73.

7. J. Riley-Smith, *The Knights of St. John in Jerusalem and Cyprus: c. 1050-1310* (London, 1967), pp. 198-226.

8. Luttrell, *Hospitallers in Cyprus, Rhodes...*, I, 282-284; *idem, Latin Greece...*, I, 250; VI, 81-82. /Editor's note: these works reprint previously published articles, cited by *chapter* and page hereafter as (e.g.) I, 282-284./

9. R. de Mas Latrie (ed.), *Chroniques de Chypre d'Amadi et de Strambaldi*, 2 vols. (Paris, 1891-1893), I, 238; Florio Bustron, *Chronique de L'Île de Chypre*, ed. R. de Mas Latrie (Paris, 1886), p. 134.

10. Zachariadou, *Trade and Crusade...*, pp. 10-11. There is widespread disagreement in the sources as to whether the conquest ended in 1309 or 1310; possibly Rhodes capitulated in August 1309 while other operations were completed in 1310. One copy of the statutes, written just after 1330 in Toulouse, Archives Départementales de la Haute-Garonne, H (Malte), 10, fol. 27, recorded, somewhat obscurely or corruptly, a decision of 1315: *Item establit es que mosey/nor/ lo maestre /per sens/ especial gracia totas las despessas faychas per raso de la guerra de Rodas del comensamen tro a la presa del castel de Rodas sals que daytant aretengut que se deia contar en .l. m. florins dau/r/ cascun an los quals se deuon contar sobrel thesaur aysi cum solian despendre en chipre per la couen los quals son en somme contes per els a per nos c. l. iiij. m. e. v. florins daur.* 50.000 florins a year for three years, i.e. until mid-1309, would have made roughly 154.005 (or 154,500?) florins, which the Convent apparently owed to the Master.

11. Zachariadou, *Trade and Crusade...*, pp. 11-12; Luttrell, *The Later History...*, pp. 143; 158, n. 6; see also B. Kedar — S. Schein, "Un Projet de *Passage Particulier* proposé par l'Ordre de l'Hôpital: 1306-1307," *Bibliothèque de l'École des Chartes*, CXXXVII (1979), and N. Housley, "Pope Clement V and the Crusades of 1309-10," in *Journal of Medieval History*, VIII (1982).

12. *Istoria del Regno di Romania*, in C. Hopf, *Chroniques Gréco-Romanes inédits ou peu connues* (Berlin, 1873), p. 167; the identity of *Strumbrachi* remains obscure.

13. Delaville, *Les Hospitaliers à Rhodes...*, pp. 10-11; Luttrell, *Hospitallers in Cyprus, Rhodes...*, I, 286-287; V, 196-197, 202; and text in L. de Mas Latrie, *Histoire de l'Île de Chypre sous le Règne des Princes de la Maison de Lusignan*, 3 vols. (Paris, 1852-1855, 1861), II, 118-125; cf. J. Richard, "Le Royaume de Chypre et l'Embargo sur le Commerce avec l'Égypte (fin XIIIe - début XIVe Siècle)," in *Académie des Inscriptions et Belles-Lettres: Comptes Rendus* (1984), and B. Kedar, "L'*Officium Robarie* di Genova: un Tentativo do coesistere con la Violenza," *Archivio Storico Italiano*, CXLIII (1985). Amadi in *Chroniques de Chypre...*, p. 395, dated the capture of two Genoese galleys and other ships sailing from Cyprus to Genoa and the imprisonment of their merchants to 25 May 1313.

14. Cf. J. Hillgarth, *Ramon Lull and Lullism in Fourteenth-Century France* (Oxford, 1971), pp. 77-78, 86-87, 93, 100-101, 104-106 *et passim*.

15. Text in E. Müller, *Das Konzil von Vienne: 1311-1312* (Münster-in-Westfalen, 1934), pp. 703-704.

16. Texts and discussion in *ibid*, pp. 226-232, 651-652, 682-703. The extent of the protests and of the papal response went further than is generally noted; this theme requires further study. In 1308 and 1309 the pope was already granting the Hospital various Templar monies in Cyprus and the administration of their properties there; Riley-Smith, *Knights of St. John...*, p. 219.

17. Luttrell, *Hospitallers in Cyprus, Rhodes...*, II, 756; *idem, Latin Greece...*, I, 251-252; *idem*, "Notes on Foulques de Villaret, Master of the Hospital 1305-1319," in *Guillaume de Villaret Ier Recteur du Comtat Venaissin 1274 Grand Maître de l'Order des Hospitaliers de Saint-Jean de Jérusalem Chypre 1296* (Paris, 1985); cf. M. Barber, *The Trial of the Templars* (Cambridge, 1978), pp. 227-231. There had, of course, been numerous Latin-Mamluk truces before 1291.

18. Amadi in *Chroniques de Chypre...*, p. 393.

19. Text cited in Luttrell, *Hospitallers in Cyprus, Rhodes...*, III, 756, n. 3.

20. Ludolph of Sudheim, *De Itinere Terrae Sanctae Liber*, ed. F. Deycks (Stuttgart, 1851), pp. 28-29; the battle is dated to the period of Villaret's deposition (1317-1319).

21. Amadi in *Chroniques de Chypre...*, p. 400.

22. Text in Delaville, *Les Hospitaliers à Rhodes...*, pp. 365-367.

23. Giovanni Villani, *Cronica*, ed. F. Dragomanni (Florence, 1845), II, 224; no contemporary source named this island. Zachariadou, *Trade and Crusade...*, p. 14, n. 5, and others suggest that Villani's *isoletta* near Rhodes was Episkope.

24. G. Neumann, "Ludolphus de Sudheim, De Itinere Terre Sancte," *Archives de l'Orient Latin*, II (1884), 333-334.

25. The dates remain uncertain: Luttrell, *Hospitallers in Cyprus, Rhodes...*, XXV, 1; *idem, Latin Greece...*, I, 253; Zachariadou, *Trade and Crusade...*, pp. 13-14.

26. Luttrell, *Latin Greece...*, VI, 86-87. 300 Turks defending Phileremos on Rhodes were put to the sword in 1306: G. Raynaud (ed.), *Les Gestes des Chiprois* (Geneva, 1887), p. 321.

27. Riley-Smith, *Knights of St. John...*, p. 88. The Templar survivors were killed at Acre in 1291: *ibid.*, p. 187. The Templars' Syrian sergeants were all beheaded by the Mamluks when taken at Ruad in 1303, though the captured Templar brethren were spared: Raynaud (ed.), *Gestes des Chiprois*, p. 310.

28. Zachariadou, *Trade and Crusade...*, pp. 13-20.

29. Luttrell, *Hospitallers in Cyprus, Rhodes...*, III, 759-761.

30. Zachariadou, *Trade and Crusade...*, p. 13, n. 50; Delaville, *Les Hospitaliers à Rhodes...*, p. 8, mistakenly writes of it as being in Ottoman hands.

31. Ludolph of Sudheim, *De Itinere...*, p. 28. There was a Hospitaller Com-

mander of Kos by 1337: Valletta, National Library of Malta, Archives of the Order of St. John, Cod. 280, fol. 39v.

32. Luttrell, *Hospitallers in Cyprus, Rhodes...*, III; *idem*, "Settlement on Rhodes: 1306-1366," in *Crusade and Settlement*, ed. P. Edbury (Cardiff, 1985).

33. Zachariadou, *Trade and Crusade...*, p. 17, n. 66. According to *Iohannis Cantacuzeni eximperatoris Historiarum Libri IV*, ed. L. Schopen, 3 vols. (Bonn, 1828-1832), I, 380-385, when in 1329 the Byzantines were expelling the Zaccaria from Chios, the Hospitallers seem first to have provided a garrison and subsequently to have sent a mission, presumably with a view to recovering Chios for the Latins, perhaps even for the Hospital.

34. Setton, *Papacy and Levant...*, I, 180, n. 8.

35. Zachariadou, *Trade and Crusade...*, pp. 24-33.

35. The two somewhat conflicting sources are Ioannes Cantacuzenus, *Historiarum Libri IV...*, I, 477-478, and *Nicephori Gregorae, Byzantina Historia*, ed. L. Schopen, 2 vols (Bonn, 1829-1830), I, 525-526, 531; Zachariadou, *Trade and Crusade...*, pp. 24-25, n. 91 and pp. 38-39, provides the background and interpretation, and the tentative dating followed here; amend the brief account in Luttrell, *Hospitallers in Cyprus, Rhodes...*, I, 293 and n. 26.

37. Luttrell, *Hospitallers in Cyprus, Rhodes...*, I, 293-294; VIII, 317-319; *idem, Latin Greece...*, I, 252-253; XVI, 133-135; see also Zachariadou, *Trade and Crusade...*, pp. 33-37.

38. Text in E. Déprez *et al.* (eds.), *Clément VI (1342-1352): Lettres closes, patentes et curiales se rapportant à la France*, I, fasc. 1 (Paris, 1901), no. 341; Luttrell, *Hospitallers in Cyprus, Rhodes...*, XXIV, summarizes other judgments on the Hospital.

39. Ludolph of Sudheim, *De Itinere...*, pp. 27-28; Neumann (ed.), "Ludolphus de Sudheim...," 333-334. The phrase concerning Turkish tribute did not appear in the later, variant manuscripts, possibly because it was no longer being paid.

40. ...*omnia capitula et conuentiones, quas habemus in ueteri sacramentali cum Hospitale*: text of 1348 in Zachariadou, *Trade and Crusade...*, pp. 205-210.

41. *Nicephori Gregorae Byzantina Historia*, II, 597.

42. Setton, *Papacy and Levant...*, I, 186, 190-194, 202-205, 208-209, 218, 223; according to Ducas, *Istoria Turco-Bizantină: 1341-1462*, ed. V. Grecu (Bucharest, 1958), translated as Doukas, *Decline and Fall of Byzantium to the Ottoman Turks*, trans. H. Magoulias (Detroit, 1975), vii:2-3, it was the Hospitallers who had built a fleet and who constructed and defended the fortress so that fugitive Christians could escape the Turks.

43. *Lo mastro dello spidale de Rodi vetava chelle navi de Veneziani non venissino, anche mannava lo fodero elie arme alli Turchi*: Anonimo Romano, *Cronica*, ed. G. Porta (Milan, 1979), p. 117.

44. Luttrell, *Hospitallers in Cyprus, Rhodes...*, V, 203-204; VI, 171-174.

45. Zachariadou, *Trade and Crusade...*, p. 53, suggests convincingly that a truce between Khizir and a contracting party which had "islands, ports, castles" was made with the Hospital in 1346; Greek text in *ibid.*, pp. 201-204.

46. Cf. Setton, *Papacy and Levant...*, I, 192, n. 154; 202, n. 45; 207-208.

47. Luttrell, *Hospitallers in Cyprus, Rhodes...*, V. 203-205; Setton, *Papacy and Levant...*, I, 208-223; Zachariadou, *Trade and Crusade...*, pp. 41-60. Housley, *Avignon Papacy and Crusades...*, pp. 301-309, studies the government of Smyrna from 1344 to 1378.

48. Luttrell, *Hospitallers in Cyprus, Rhodes...*, I and XXIV.

49. Philip of Mézières, *Le Songe du vieil Pèlerin*, ed. G. Coopland, 2 vols. (Cambridge, 1969), I, 259-260.

50. Zachariadou, *Trade and Crusade...*, pp. 60-62, 66, 71-75. In about 1359 a Hospitaller force helped to destroy thirty-five Turkish ships off Megara: Luttrell, *Hospitallers in Cyprus, Rhodes...*, V, 206, n. 115.

51. J. Smet (ed.), *The Life of Saint Peter Thomas by Philippe de Mézières* (Rome, 1954), pp. 85-86.

52. Delaville, *Les Hospitaliers à Rhodes...*, p. 141.

53. Mézières, *Peter Thomas*, p. 127; Leontios Makhairas, *Recital concerning the Sweet Land of Cyprus entitled "Chronicle,"* ed. and trans. R. Dawkins, 2 vols. (Oxford, 1932), I, 148-149, 168-177, 180-183. The Hospitallers were close to King Pierre at Alexandria — *Le roi estoit sus son cheval, /Et les freres de l'Ospital/ Environ lui, trestous ensamble*: Guillaume de Machaut, *La Prise d'Alexandrie*, ed. L. de Mas Latrie (Geneva, 1877), p. 87.

54. Text in P. Riant, "Six Lettres relative aux Croisades," *Archives de l'Orient Latin* (1881), I, 391-392; see also Zachariadou, *Trade and Crusade...*, pp. 69-70.

55. On 4 December 1365 the Master ordered the purchase in Apulia of 1000 horses and of quantities of victuals *que de Turquia unde illa haberj consueverant ad presens habere non possunt, adeo indignati sunt Turchi propter Alexandrie invasionem*: Malta, Cod. 319, fol. 316.

56. Luttrell, *Hospitallers in Cyprus, Rhodes...*, XXII, 35; M. Hayez (ed.), *Urbain V (1362-1370): Lettres Communes*, 2 vols. (Paris, 1964-1971), II, no. 6420; it is hard to establish how much weight should be given to standard repetitions of references to incursions, devastations, and depopulations in papal bulls granting such privileges.

57. Malta, Cod. 48, fols. 63v, 64, 223v-224.

58. *Infra,...*

59. Luttrell, *Latin Greece...*, I, 257-259; A.-M. Legras, "Les Effectifs de l'Ordre des Hospitaliers de Saint-Jean de Jérusalem dans le Prieuré de France en 1373," *Revue Mabillon*, LX (1984).

60. Luttrell, *Latin Greece...*, XV.

61. Text in J. Miret y Sans, *Les Cases de Templers y Hospitallers en Catalunya* (Barcelona, 1910), pp. 456-458.

62. Delaville, *Les Hospitaliers à Rhodes...*, pp. 215, 384-386; Luttrell, *Hospitallers in Cyprus, Rhodes...*, XXII; idem, "Le Schisme dans les Prieurés de l'Hôpital en Catalunya et Aragón," *Jornades sobre el Cisma d'Occident a Catalunya, les illes i el país valencià*, I (Barcelona, 1986).

63. W. Müller-Wiener, "Die Stadtbefestigung von Ismir, Siğacik und Çandarli: Bemerkungen zur mittelalterlichen Topographie des nördlichen Jonien," *Istanbuler Mitteilungen*, XII (1962).

64. Doukas, *Decline and Fall...*, xiii:2; xvii:2. Bayezid attacked Smyrna repeatedly, according to Doukas, xvii:2; Cherefeddin Ali, *Histoire de Timur-Bec*, trans. F. Pétis de la Croix, IV (Paris, 1722), 45, 53; and Andrea de Reduciis, *Chronicon Tarvisinum* in L. Muratori, *Rerum Italicarum Scriptores*, XIX (Milan, 1731), 801.

65. Delaville, *Les Hospitaliers à Rhodes...*, pp. 229-230.

66. Luttrell, *The Later History...*, p. 158, nn. 11-12.

67. Malta, Cod. 326, fol. 147v.

68. Malta, Cod. 327, fol. 25.

69. Text in Zachariadou, *Trade and Crusade...*, p. 210.

70. E. Legrand (ed.), "Relation du Pèlerinage à Jérusalem de Nicolas de Martoni, Notaire italien: 1394-1395," *Revue de l'Orient Latin*, III (1895), 582, 639.

71. Genoa, Archivio di Stato, Sezione Notai: Donato de Chiavari, nos. 169-172.

72. Setton, *Papacy and Levant...*, I, 356.

73. Text in J. Barker, *Manuel II Palaeologus 1391-1425: a Study in Late Byzantine Statesmanship* (New Brunswick, 1969), pp. 482-483.

74. Setton, *Papacy and Levant...*, I, 360, 364-366, 371.

75. C. Marinescu, "Du Nouveau sur *Tirant lo Blanch*," *Estudis Romànics*, IV (1953-1954), 139-156, 197-198.

76. Details in Luttrell, *Notes and Documents.../forthcoming/*; see also G. Hill, *A History of Cyprus*, 4 vols. (Cambridge, 1940-1952), II, 439-440.

77. Text and discussion in G. Majeska, *Russian Travellers to Constantinople in the Fourteenth and Fifteenth Centuries* (Washington, 1984), pp. 102-103, 411, 413; Barker, *Manuel II...*, p. 77, gives the number of galleys as two.

78. Luttrell, *Latin Greece...*, XI, 242-247; R.-J. Loenertz, *Byzantina et Franco-Graeca* (Rome, 1970), pp. 254-264; J. Chrysostomides (ed.), *Manuel II Palaeologus Funeral Oration on his Brother Theodore* (Thessalonika, 1985), pp. 20-24, 166-210.

79. Text of a letter from Bonacorso Grimani, dated Rhodes, 20 April 1403, in Venice, Biblioteca Marciana, Ms. Latini, Classe X, 299 /3512/, fols. 65-67v; this text will be republished in Luttrell, *Notes and Documents... /forthcoming/*.

80. Delaville, *Les Hospitaliers à Rhodes...*, pp. 284-285; Luttrell, *Notes and Documents... /forthcoming/*.

81. Text in F. Thiriet, *Duca di Candia — Ducali e Lettere ricevuti: 1358-1360; 1401-1405* (Venice, 1978), p. 37.

82. Cherefeddin Ali, *Histoire de Timur-Bec*, IV, 50, 56.

83. *Ibid.*, IV, 46-53.

84. An Italian inhabitant of Damascus, Beltramo Mignanelli, *Vita Tamerlani*,

in S. Baluze, *Miscellanea*, ed. J. Mansi, IV (Lucca, 1764), 139, wrote that the Hospitallers surrendered by pact; details and discussion in Luttrell, *Notes and Documents*... /forthcoming/.

85. Luttrell, *The Later History*..., p. 143.

86. F. López Estrada (ed.), *Embajada a Tamorlán* (Madrid, 1943), pp. 22-24; the garrison at Kos is unlikely to have been composed of 100 Hospitallers, as the text stated.

87. Text cited *supra*, note 79.

88. G. Dennis, "The Byzantine-Turkish Treaty of 1403," *Orientalia Christiana Periodica*, XXXIII (1967).

89. Luttrell, *Notes and Documents*... /forthcoming/.

90. Text in P. Schriener, *Die Byzantinischen Kleinchroniken*, I (Vienna, 1975), 345.

91. Chrysostomides (ed.), *Manuel II*..., pp. 23-24, 208.

92. Setton, *Papacy and Levant*..., I, 384-388.

93. Luttrell, *The Later History*..., pp. 144-145.

94. Doukas, *Decline and Fall*..., xviii:3-11; xxi:2, 4-5; xxii:1; discussion and chronology in Luttrell, *The Later History*..., pp. 144-145.

95. According to Doukas, *Decline and Fall*..., xxii:1.

96. The sources may be unreliable on this point: Luttrell, *The Later History*..., pp. 144-146.

97. Luttrell, *The Later History*..., pp. 145-146.

98. As claimed, among others, by Delaville, *Les Hospitaliers à Rhodes*..., p. 287.

99. Details in Luttrell, *The Later History*..., pp. 146-147; 150; 159, n. 29; the earliest Hospitaller occupation and fortification at Bodrum are dicussed *ibid.*, pp. 149-156.

100. Malta, Cod. 333, fol. 245v.

101. Malta, Cod. 333, fols. 267v-268, 271, 271v.

102. Malta, Cod. 339, fols. 213v, 289, 298v; while these seem to be the earliest documents concerning the Rhodian *corso* to survive, the institution may well have been older.

103. Details in Luttrell, *The Later History*..., pp. 147; 159, nn. 40-50. It seems that Mehmet did attack Junayd at Smyrna and ask for Hospitaller help in 1415, and that Doukas knew this but mistakenly recounted the incident of ca. 1407, when Mehmet at Smyrna awarded Bodrum to the Hospital, as if it too occurred in 1415: cf. *ibid*, pp. 144-147. The Hospital's accounts for October 1410 noted a mission to Suleyman *in partibus turquie* by Fr. *Stolonus* de Lescure: Malta, Cod. 339, fols. 168v-170.

104. Malta, Cod. 339, fols. 125, 168v-170, 176, 291v.

105. Malta, Cod. 339, fol. 296.

106. Malta, Cod. 346, fol. 169v, published, inaccurately, in E. Gerland, *Neue Quellen zur Geschichte des Lateinischen Erzbistums Patras* (Leipzig, 1903), pp. 171-173. Junayd returned to Smyrna and retook Ephesus and other territories early in 1422: Doukas, *Decline and Fall...*, xxvi:4.

107. Luttrell, *Hospitallers in Cyprus, Rhodes...*, IV, 57-58.

108. W. Paravicini, "Financer la Croisade continuelle: Voyage de Prusse et Guerre contre les Lithuaniens au XIVe Siècle" /forthcoming/.

109. Text in L. Toulmin Smith, *Expedition to Prussia and the Holy Land made by Henry, Earl of Derby...*, (London, 1894), pp. 227, 283.

110. Luttrell, *The Later History...*, pp. 150; 159, n. 29; A. Reeves, *Lancastrian Englishmen* (Washington, 1981), p. 81.

111. Cf. J. Woś, "Le Origine del Conflitto fra Ordine Teutonico e Regno Polacco e il Problema della *Guerra Giusta,*" in his *Dispute Giuridiche nella Lotta fra la Polonia e l'Ordine Teutonico* (Florence, 1979); E. Christiansen, *The Northern Crusade — The Baltic and the Catholic Frontier: 1100-1525* (London, 1980), pp. 219-232.

112. Delaville, *Les Hospitaliers à Rhodes...*, pp. 323-325.

113. M. Burleigh, *Prussian Society and the German Order: an Aristocratic Corporation in Crisis, c. 1410-1466* (Cambridge, 1984).

114. Doukas, *Decline and Fall...*, xliii:2. The Hospital had, however, offered tribute to the Egyptians in 1427: A. Darrag, *L'Égypte sous le Règne de Barsbay: 825-841/1422-1438* (Damascus, 1961), p. 264.

CHRISTIANITY AND SCIENCE IN LATE MING CHINA:
Jesuit Missionaries and the Conversion of the Literati

Charlton M. Lewis

I. Introduction

During the late sixteenth and early seventeenth centuries—the era of Queen Elizabeth, the Spanish Armada, Galileo, and Shakespeare—a small force of Jesuit missionaries began a crusade to evangelize the Chinese. It was a climactic period in the history of Christianity. Already Catholic missionaries had ridden the wave of European expansion, accompanying Spanish conquistadors to the West Indies, Mexico, and Peru, and Portuguese merchants to Africa, India, and the Spice Islands of the East. By the 1550s they were preaching in Malacca, Japan, and Macao, and by the 1560s in the Philippines. As the global network of European trade spread, the Chinese were increasingly drawn in. The annual voyages of the Manila Galleons across the Pacific, begun in 1565, attracted fleets of Chinese junks to the Philippine entrepôt. Silver from the Spanish empire in the Americas flowed westward, while Chinese silks and porcelains enriched the lives of Spanish aristocrats in Mexico. Early Jesuit missionaries such as Francis Xavier, who died while trying to gain entry to China in 1552, and Allesandro Valignano, who shaped Jesuit policies in Asia for three decades before his death in 1606, responded to the challenge of what they rightly discerned to be one of the world's great empires. By the time Matteo Ricci, the pioneer missionary in China, died in Beijing in 1610, there were some 2500 Chinese converts under 16 Jesuit missionaries;[1] the crusade was underway.

The Jesuit mission may not have greatly influenced the course of Chinese history, but it is well worth our attention as an instance of cultural diffusion from Europe to Eastern Asia. Few proselytizers in history can have been so able, so persistent, or so conscious of their roles as emissaries from another world. Their hopes were spurred during the late Ming, not so much by total numbers of converts (no more than 70,000 by 1640)[2] as by their success among the elite, many from the literati. By 1636 Christian converts included 14 high officials and numerous holders of civil service degrees (10 *jinshi*, 11 *juren*, and 251 *xiucai*); also, more than 140 relatives of the imperial family, more than 40 eunuchs in the imperial service, and several "great ladies" were converts.[3] This Christian success among the top echelons of Chinese society was unique in history before the twentieth century. Even during the heyday of the mission in the Kangxi period (1662-1722), when the Jesuits were close to the Qing court, they could not claim many of the eminent among their converts.

Why particularly in the late Ming did the Jesuits, as a cultural elite from Europe, succeed in popularizing their teachings among the cultural elite in China? One reason is that the Jesuits skillfully accommodated themselves to the Chinese world. Experiences in India and Japan had taught them that their message of redemption and salvation, baldly delivered, would make little sense to the Chinese. They therefore posed not merely as representatives of the Vatican, but as worldly emissaries from Renaissance Europe. They offered their skills in what we may loosely call science — mathematics, astronomy, surveying, cartography, hydraulics, and even military technology — whatever might serve the needs of a large, sophisticated, agrarian civilization and make their religious teachings more palatable. Thus Christianity came into China as merely one of an array of cultural attributes from Europe. A second reason may be that the late Ming period (roughly 1550-1644) was particularly open to the combination of ideas that the Jesuits brought with them. To study the experience of Christianity in the Chinese world helps us to appreciate the importance of cultural context for all religions in all times and places. It also helps us to understand how ideas change their meanings as they move from one human environment to another.

This article explores the ways in which Jesuit teachings on Christianity and science fitted into the mental world of the Chinese educated elite in the late Ming period. It shows that their ideas in these areas of knowledge were regarded by Chinese as parts of a unified whole, so that "religion" and "science" were not distinguished from each other. It argues that the Jesuit teachings, to the extent that they were accepted in late Ming China, remained little more than useful elaborations of concepts already central to the Confucian order. If this interpretation is correct, it helps us to understand the strength and resiliency of Chinese civilization, and why Western Christianity and science have both remained marginal among educated Chinese down to the twentieth century.

II. The Jesuit Enterprise

The Jesuit order represented Catholicism in a new key, a burning intensity of faith, blended with the militancy, sophistication, and intellectual achievement of Renaissance and post-Renaissance Europe. Ignatius Loyola (1491-1556), the Basque soldier and mystic who founded the Society of Jesus, gave it its combative, authoritarian character and its emphasis on hard work in the world. (His *Spiritual Exercises* stressed obedience and mastery of the will, not religious doctrine.) Its humanistic emphasis on education grew logically from the urge to "propagate the faith" among the elite who controlled the religious destinies of European states. Beginning as a ministry to the poor, first to illiterate children in Italian parishes and then to advanced students through a network of colleges, the Jesuits quickly became teachers to many among the upper classes of Catholic Europe. [4] More than other orders of the day, they combined the idealistic and the practical, the emotional and the rational, religious zeal and an instinct for power. This fusion of opposing tendencies strengthened their evangelical mission and served them well in China.

Concentration on the elite fitted the political needs of the time. In an age of sectarian division, religious uniformity was widely viewed as crucial for political stability. This principle, which became the basis for settlement of religious conflict in Europe, required that ecclesiastical leaders work closely with local rulers. Soon the same principle was extended to the mission fields. King John III of Portugal, who sent Francis Xavier and other early Jesuits out from Lisbon in 1541, exhorted them to convert the aristocrats, and through them to make wholesale conversions. [5]

Reaching the elite in South Asia and Japan proved difficult, however, and experiences there further prepared the Jesuits for their approach to China. Led by Xavier, they soon dominated the *padroado*, the system by which the Portuguese monarch controlled ecclesiastical patronage within his empire. The biggest question that they confronted was how far to accommodate themselves to native language and custom. Once outside the Portuguese-occupied colony of Goa, officials of the *padroado* could not use the forceful tactics that had sometimes been employed against Muslims or Jews in Spain and Africa. With their humanistic background and broad educations, the Jesuits were drawn to study the languages and cultures of the areas they hoped to evangelize. Although they gained little knowledge of classical literatures, they gradually learned to translate simple prayers and catechisms into Tamil, Malay, Japanese, and other languages, and to promulgate them through churches and schools. [6]

More complex was the question of whether to permit converts to conduct traditional "rites" or practices that seemed inconsistent with Christian teachings. Should a Brahmin who professed Christianity be permitted to wear his Brahmin thread? [7] Should Japanese converts be allowed to continue customs and ceremonies that were used by Buddhist priests? [8] It was Allesandro Valignano, a Neapolitan aristocrat who was sent to Goa in 1574 as visitor for the Asian mission, who made such accommodations a firm policy for Jesuits. A holder of a doctorate in law from the University of Padua, Valignano brought a humanistic sensibility to the field. Concentrating on the Japanese and Chinese, whom he believed to be intellectually superior to Indians, he advocated study of their languages and customs as the surest means to win the respect and confidence of their elites. In Japan, where he arrived in 1579, he inaugurated a policy of flexible adaptation to local custom, instituting language training, schools, seminaries for native clergy, and a printing press to try to introduce Western and Christian literature to the country. In Macao, he initiated similar forms of cultural accommodation. Instead of "Portugalizing" converts by having them take Portuguese names, wear Portuguese clothes, and learn the Portuguese language, he ordered missionaries to "Sinicize" themselves by studying Chinese, wearing Chinese clothes, and imitating Chinese customs. It was he who first brought a missionary, Michele Ruggieri, to Macao to learn Chinese for the specific purpose of gaining entrance to China. [9]

The policy of cultural accommodation required intelligent and resilient leaders who could adapt to the languages and ways of an alien people. Evangelization by the book was not enough. As the vice-provincial, Father Anton de Quadros, wrote in 1566, it was better to have fewer priests carefully selected than many of poor quality, for the "East is not a school for training novices." [10] After the Council of Trent stiffened requirements for clerical training, Jesuit colleges in Portugal could no longer provide enough men of learning and stature for the expanding missionary fields in Asia and Brazil. The Portuguese *padroado* was soon admitting missionaries from other European countries, and Italian Jesuits, many of them supremely well-educated and skilled, assumed leading positions. Among them were Valignano and Matteo Ricci, who pioneered the China mission.

From the beginning, the China mission required delicate tactics. The Portuguese commercial empire within which the Jesuits worked was dependent on the good will of Chinese officials. Moreover, the Jesuits themselves, to secure their mission financially, had invested heavily in the silk trade and could not afford to arouse Chinese anger. [11] Michele Ruggieri, the first Jesuit admitted to China, gained permission to reside at Zhaoqing near Canton (1582) because his good manners and diplomatic skills had impressed the governor-general. [12] Ruggieri was soon joined by Ricci, also a man of delicate tact. As the mission expanded, first to Shaozhou (north of Canton), then to Nanchang and Nanjing in central China, and finally to Beijing, where Ricci died in 1610, he and his colleagues slowly worked out ways to gain support from influential Chinese.

The Jesuits in China developed a three-fold approach. One component of their strategy, expanding from ideas of Xavier and Valignano, was to immerse themselves in Chinese cultural life. Language study remained their first priority, not merely colloquial dialects but classical written texts. Language in turn opened to them the world of philosophical discourse through reading, writing, and discussion. They quickly perceived the importance of literature in China, the lavish attention given to printing, ink mixing, and seal carving, and the prestige accorded to men of letters. Ricci and many others made empire-wide reputations by publishing essays and tracts, some in the humanistic vein of Erasmus or Montaigne, others on religious subjects. They cultivated the manner of the *junzi* (superior man), the Confucian ideal of the self-disciplined esthete with stern morality and great intellectual style. Ricci drew on the mnemonic devices popular in Europe to help him study Chinese ideographs, and later won admiration from Chinese literati for his ability to memorize pages of Chinese text. [13]

Second, the Jesuits attempted to accommodate their Christianity to Chinese language, traditions, and practices. Such accommodation was difficult because the Chinese cosmology had no counterpart of a transcendent, Creator God who shaped man's destiny. Confucianism and Buddhism offered no vision of a permanent afterlife or any conception of sin and redemption. The mere translation of the Latin word *Deus* was a major problem. Terms such as *shangdi* (the sovereign above), *Tian* (Heaven), *shen* (spirit) or *Taiji* (Supreme Ultimate), as used in antiquity, had in certain contexts suggested personhood or transcendence. But in the Neo-Confucian world of the late Ming period, they had more metaphysical connotations, suggesting ultimate principle, or immanence of spirit. Ricci and others finally decided on the artificial term, *Tianzhu* (Lord of Heaven), but the question of appropriate translations of Christian terms was never fully settled. A more serious problem was whether to permit Chinese Christians to observe Confucian ancestral rites, the ritualized respect for the family dead whose shades lingered in the spirit world and influenced the destiny of the household. Here Ricci prevailed over his less flexible colleagues, stressing "the accommodation of the practice of the Christian religion — not its contents — to the particular Chinese conditions." [14]

The third component of the Jesuit approach was to impress the Chinese with the superiority of Western civilization, to convince them that Europe was an ideal society that proved Christianity to be a worthy doctrine. Through their writings in Chinese, the missionaries worked to create a halcyon image of Europe in ways that were sometimes quite unscrupulous. On an influential map of the world that he first published in 1584, Ricci described the countries of Europe as prosperous, happy monarchies which "do not embrace any other religion but Catholicism." The people "are solid and honest, and have a high regard for the five relationships" (the Confucian prescription for an ordered society). He did not mention the Protestant Reformation or the religious wars. [15] Giulio Aleni, one of the most prolific Jesuit writers in Chinese, wrote in 1637 that European kings "are all connected by marriage, and therefore live on good terms with one another," that in case of war the pope intervenes ("He sends out envoys to warn the belligerents to stop fighting"), that the "Five Constant Relations are honored in every righteous country," that bandits are rare, that there are no whippings or floggings in the prisons, that "ceremonies for the ancestors are very important," and that European traders are always accompanied by educated men. "As soon as they arrive in a given country, they learn its language and literature, follow the local dressing and eating habits, and observe the local customs. Then they teach the people with all their heart." [16]

More directly, the Jesuits sought to demonstrate European superiority in technology and science. Spring-wound clocks, some of which sounded bells, played melodies, or paraded little automatic figures, were gifts coveted by Chinese as marks of status. [17] So were musical instruments, crystal mirrors, prisms, eyeglasses, and other exotic items, which the missionaries used as presents. Ricci had studied with Christopher Clavius (1534-1612), the German Jesuit

who had helped create the reformed Gregorian Calendar.
He and his colleagues taught mathematics to Confucian
scholars, and with their aid published books on Western
geometry, surveying, cartography, and calendar calculation. Given Jesuit objectives in China, it is not surprising
that Christianity and science went hand in hand, nor should
we read back from our own times the presumption that religion and science belong in separate domains. In Europe,
prior to Descartes, there was no perceived conflict between
Christian truth and scientific truth. As A. R. Hall writes,
"a very high proportion of scientists up to the mid-seven-
teenth century were men of unusually profound religious
conviction.../and/ the furtherance of science and religion
were commonly regarded as inseparable objectives.[18] In
using science to bolster their Christian message, the Jesuits
saw no conflict at all. Their easy blend of Christian and
scientific truth fitted readily into the Chinese intellectual
world that they had entered, and contributed to their successful conversions among educated Chinese.

III. Late Ming: An Eclectic Age

Late Ming China was a restless and inquiring age, in
some respects similar to the European world from which the
Jesuits had come. Political stagnation, commercial growth,
and social disequilibrium had created a pervasive sense of
disorder. Cultural and intellectual life was eclectic, quest-
ing, and intense. By examining this environment we can
gain perspective on why some educated Chinese responded
favorably to Jesuit ideas on religion and science.

Paralysis in the central administration was a source of
gathering anxiety for the scholar elite. The Wanli Emperor
(r. 1573-1620), whose reign dominated the late Ming, was
a truculent and extravagant recluse. Inaction at the top of
the Ming autocracy enabled eunuchs to usurp imperial
functions and thwarted able officials in their efforts to conduct government. Corruption and factionalism were rife,
aggravated by lavish spending, outbreaks of rebellion, and
external threats. During its last three decades the dynasty
could do little to impede the expanding Manchu state in
the northeast.

Social and economic changes were causing new tensions. The population may have doubled during the sixteenth century to about 150 million while the economy was becoming more commercialized. Expanding cotton and silk industries in the Yangtze Valley had created a rich inter-regional trade, and the riverine cities teemed with wealthy merchants and talented artisans. Rising production and the opening of European trade stimulated commerce abroad. Dozens of large sea junks traded annually at Manila, which by 1586 had a Chinese community of 10,000.[19] Silver, in part imported from Spanish America, became the basis for a growing money economy, while government mining enterprises created further opportunities for wealth and corruption.

As in Europe, an urban proto-bourgeoisie aspired to scholarly tastes and influenced styles in art and literature. Rich merchants became art patrons and contributed to the prestige of literati artists.[20] Ming landscape painting developed a new assymetry of "almost painful distortions," perhaps expressing the social tensions of the age.[21] Printing was simple, efficient, and widespread. Vast numbers of books, many with illustrations, circulated at low prices and became a medium for European cultural diffusion. This was a golden age for colloquial fiction — short stories and novels — written for an affluent urban clientele. The splendid decadence of literary taste (some of it highly erotic) breached the walls of Confucian orthodoxy, even as the civil service examinations, with their narrow and rigid eight-legged essays, were becoming more formalistic.[22] Many educated men were distressed by the moral emptiness of contemporary writing. Xu Guangqi, a high official and Christian convert, criticized the productions of "literary gentlemen," which were "written with flourishes and argued with elegance," but were of no more value than "engraving on fat or carving on ice."[23]

In other parallels to the European Renaissance, scholars such as Wang Shizhen (1526-1590) sought to return to ancient styles of writing.[24] Mei Zu (ca. 1543) and Shen Defu (1578-1642) developed a more critical attitude toward the past, making careful use of primary sources and discovering forgeries in hallowed classics.[25] Private academies flourished, in what Hucker has called "an academy craze," where groups of scholars outside the government discussed values and politics.[26]

What qualities in the late Ming philosophical milieu impelled members of the scholar elite toward Western Christianity and science? The question is extremely complex, especially since so little is now known about the intellectual ferment of the period, but clues may be contained in some of the main developments of late Ming thought. These include a reaffirmation of Neo-Confucian orthodoxy, an upsurge of religious fervor, the revival of practical studies (*shixue*), and a conscious tendency to syncretism. Taken together, these developments reveal the wide diversity and tolerance of the late Ming, and the intricate relationship between moral idealism and worldly practicality that is found in the ideas of many thinkers of the period. They thus offer a framework within which we can understand the appeal of Jesuit teachings for at least some literati.

Orthodoxy in the late Ming meant the School of Principle (*Lixue*), a broad term for the Neo-Confucian teachings bequeathed from the Song period by Zhu Xi (1130-1200) and his predecessors. The School of Principle had reacted to centuries of Buddhist teaching that the world was illusory and to Daoist stress on nonaction as man's central philosophical principle. It reaffirmed the significance of man by fusing human history, social morality, and the phenomena of the natural world into one universal process (the Dao). Everything in that process, it asserted, was governed by the law of being, or principle (*li*), actualized by and inseparable from the material force (*qi*), through which each thing gained its particular character. In man, principle appeared as his true nature, fundamentally in harmony with all things, but usually obscured by impurities in the material force with which each person was differently endowed. Every person's duty, then, was to discover his own true nature, to clear away the selfish desires embedded in his material force and reveal the principle within. For this purpose the School of Principle invoked the injunction of the ancient Confucian classic of *The Great Learning* that men seek to cultivate moral knowledge through the "investigation of things" (*qewu*).

Neo-Confucians differed on what was meant by the "investigation of things." Generally, however, they regarded it as a deeply serious effort to discover principle underlying all phenomena, whether palpable objects, social relationships, personal virtues, or historical events. A man developed himself morally not only through reading books but by participating actively in the physical world around him. There is a strongly rational character to the School of Principle which some scholars have viewed as favorable to science. [27] Why the School of Principle did not eventually give rise to natural science is a complex problem which need not be examined here, but we may note that writers of this school were far more concerned with problems of human affairs than with the study of the natural world. [28] For them the "investigation of things" was the answer to the moral question of how man should improve himself, not the "scientific" question of how to explain natural phenomena.

This return to a moralistic orthodoxy was stimulated by a growing reaction against another Neo-Confucian school, that of the scholar-statesman, Wang Yangming (1472-1529). Wang had rejected the "investigation of things" as a means to discover principle, and had expounded the view that one's innate knowledge (*liangzhi*) already offered a route to moral improvement. People, he wrote, must realize "that the highest good is in the mind and does not depend on any search outside." [29] This stress on intuition rather than on intellectual effort opened the way to a flourishing moral relativism and freethinking individualism, which by the last years of the sixteenth century were making many literati uneasy. As some of Wang's followers gained notoriety by their eccentric or even licentious practices, more orthodox Confucians reacted with a new idealism which was both doctrinal and political. Many sought moral improvement by keeping daily journals to record their thoughts and behavior. [30] The Donglin Academy in Jiangsu province became a center for the expression of moral concern at the degeneracy in government and among the educated class, and called for a crusade to restore moral integrity to government. [31] The Donglin movement gave practical expression to reviving orthodoxy. Its intense moral concern was in some respects congruent with that of the Jesuit missionaries.

A second and related development in late Ming thought was an upsurge of religious activity. Perhaps the social imbalances of the times aroused a quest for spiritual insight. Or perhaps the spread of literacy and the leisure of urban life contributed to an assumption that the achievement of moral perfection should not be as intellectually arduous as Neo-Confucians had held. Certainly the radical followers of Wang Yangming contributed to an atmosphere of freedom in the religious sphere. [32] In any case, by the late sixteenth century a major revival of Buddhism was taking place, evident in sculpture, in temple building, in the popularity of Buddhism at court, and in its frequent mention in *The Golden Lotus*, the most important novel of the period. [33] The same environment that nurtured Buddhism in the late Ming probably also favored the spread of Christianity. Some literati who had been Buddhists converted to Christianity, while others showed interest without converting.

Renewed moral fervor and spiritual concern were supplemented by a third development in late Ming, a revived interest in practical studies (*shixue*). In the gathering political and social crisis, a growing number of scholars sought practical solutions to administrative problems. The period saw the publication of numerous treatises on such subjects as dikes and irrigation, city defense, diagnosis of disease, plant classification, calendar calculation, grain storage and famine relief, as well as various aspects of government administration. Examples include the work of Li Shizhen (1518-1593), best known for his extraordinary pharmacopoeia, whose investigations ranged from syphilis to the sweet potato, [34] Zhu Zaiyu (1536-1611), a royal prince with interests in mathematics, music, and phonology, who proposed a method to revise the calendar; [35] Yuan Huang (*jinshi* 1586), an eminent agriculturalist; [36] and Xu Guangqi, whom we shall examine more closely below, one of several Christian converts who tried to strengthen the state through study and research in scientific fields. Much of this new interest in practical reform belonged to the Confucian tradition of statecraft scholarship (*jingshi*, or "managing the world's affairs"). It was entirely compatible with the reviving moral idealism and religious concern. Many ideas of Jesuit missionaries who introduced Western scientific knowledge along

with their Christianity, could be integrated into the framework of late Ming thought.

Finally, as in Renaissance Europe, these new developments gave rise to a conscious syncretism. Where in Europe
Pico della Mirandola and others sought correlations among
the Hebrew, Greek, and Christian traditions, in China the
religious leader Lin Zhaoen (1517-1598) developed a syncretic religion that fused Confucianism, Daoism, and Buddhism into a single system. [37] A similar syncretism was advocated by Li Zhi (1527-1602), probably the most independent thinker of the age, who derided Confucian morality and declared that "the teachings of Confucius, the Buddha, and Lao-tzu are one." [38] Buddhism itself was highly
syncretic, inwardly among its various schools and outwardly
with Confucianism and Daoism. [39] Such an intellectual
climate made it easy for educated Confucians also to be
Buddhists, or even to accept Christian beliefs. The most
eminent of the Jesuit converts, like humanistic Christians
in Europe, were persons of broad intellectual background
and interests.

IV. Xu Guangqi (1562-1633) and the Appeal of Christianity

The religious tone and syncretic style of the late Ming
period enabled Jesuit missionaries to blend into the Chinese
cultural environment with relative ease. To understand why
their message was accepted as widely as it was, however, we
must consider the converts themselves: who they were, what
values the Western religion held for them, what intellectual
presuppositions they brought to their encounters with the
new faith. The most eminent converts of the period, Xu
Guangqi (1562-1633), Li Zhizao (1565-1630), and Yang
Tingyun (1557-1627), the so-called "Three Pillars of the
Early Catholic Church," had much in common. All had
studied many years in the Confucian literary tradition, all
held the highest degree, and all were eminent scholars and
officials. All came to Christianity relatively late in life and
were baptized in middle age, Xu at 41, Li at 45, and Yang
at 55. All were notably ardent in professing their new faith.
All were deeply interested in the secular and scientific knowledge that the Jesuits brought with them from Europe. And

all had careers which entitled them to distinction apart from their alien beliefs.[40] Their conversions confirm the richness, breadth, and tolerance of late Ming intellectual life. Did Christianity fulfill for them some spiritual need that could not be fulfilled in China? Were they attracted first by Western science and only later by Christianity? How did they reconcile European Christianity and science with their Confucian training and values?

Since the Jesuit success lay in the minds of converts such as these, let us look at one of them more closely. Xu Guangqi was probably the most eminent of the three both for his devotion to Christianity and for his scientific achievements. Xu rose from penury in the suburbs of Shanghai to become one of the highest and most influential officials in the Ming government.[41] His struggles to get through the civil service examinations constitute a model of Confucian perseverance: success in the first level degree (the *xiucai*) at age 19; four failures before attaining the provincial level (*juren*) at age 35 (1597); and seven more years with at least one failure before passing the metropolitan examinations (*jinshi*) and gaining admission to the Hanlin Academy at age 42 (1604).

His encounters with Christianity and baptism into the Catholic Church were interwoven with his last years of study for the examinations. He met his first missionary in Shaozhou (Guangdong province) where he had gone to teach after his fourth examination failure. By coincidence, this was the town where Ricci had been permitted to settle in 1589. Although Ricci was away, Xu met the resident priest, Lazare Cattaneo (1560-1640), who reportedly impressed him immensely.[42] He saw Ricci for the first time in Nanjing in 1600, and was finally baptized there in 1603 by Joao da Rocha (1565-1623). The following year he at last succeeded in the metropolitan examination.

Although it has been said that the Jesuits used Western science to lure their converts to Christianity,[43] and Xu himself later became eminent for his scientific work, his conversion to the foreign faith cannot be explained so simply. Cattaneo, who first introduced him to Christianity, was not noted for his scientific or mathematical knowledge.[44] Before meeting Ricci in 1600, Xu had seen an early version of his map of the world and had known of him as a "superior

man in China, broad and penetrating in his knowledge." [45]
But overall it was Ricci's spiritual qualities more than his
mathematical or scientific skills, that first appealed to Xu.
In his preface to Euclid's *Principles of Geometry*, which he
and Ricci translated together in 1607, he divided Ricci's
learning into three aspects, the greatest being "cultivation
of self and service to Heaven." The lesser aspects, "the investigation of things and exhaustive study of principle,"
and the related field of mathematics (*xiangshu*), merely
illustrated the accuracy and practicality of his thought. [46]
Moreover, when Xu went for baptism in 1603, it was Jesuit
religious writings that were said to have stimulated him,
notably Ricci's "True Meaning of the Lord of Heaven"
(*Tianzhu shiyi*) and another tract entitled "Essential Teachings of the Lord of Heaven" (*Tianzhu jiaoyao*). He absorbed
these materials with fervor, studied determinedly for a few
days, and was finally baptized under the name of Paul. [47] The
following year, the Jesuits reported, he was so devout "that
when he received Holy Communion, he could not restrain
his tears, nor could those who saw him at the altar rail." [48]
Subsequently, Xu maintained a devout regimen in his own
household: earnest prayer morning and evening, and careful self-examination to ascertain his shortcomings and failures. [49] He converted his father and his only son, Xu Ji,
whose children perpetuated a legacy of Catholicism at the
family estate, Xujiawei (Zicawei), down to modern times.
In its outer forms and spiritual aspirations, Xu's Christianity seems close to the reformist Confucianism practiced by
many of his contemporaries. [50]

What was the appeal of Christianity to Xu? Although
he did not write extensively of his beliefs, the sources we
have indicate that he regarded the new religion as consistent
with but superior to Confucian doctrine. He was drawn to
the Jesuits as moral teachers in the Confucian style, especially to Ricci, whose words were all consistent with "the
great principles of loyalty and filial piety" and were "bene-
ficial to people's minds and the way of the world." [51] In his
defense in 1617 of certain Jesuits who had been attacked
by an anti-Christian official, he likened the missionaries
to disciples of the Confucian sages (*shengxian zhi tu*): "their
doctrine (Dao) is most correct, their discipline most strict,

their learning most extensive, their knowledge most refined,
their hearts most sincere, their viewpoints most firm; in their
own countries they are outstandingly eminent.... All their
precepts and injunctions are fully compatible with Heaven's
principle and human nature (*Tianli renqing*)." [52] Moreover, the civilization from which they came seemed to confirm the beneficent effects of Christianity. European nations had existed for centuries, he believed, well-adminis-
tered and tranquil, where personal virtue was ubiquitous:
the people "are cautious and attentive, only fearing to fall
into error and sin against the Lord of Heaven." It appears
that he was completely convinced of the veracity of Jesuit
accounts. Perhaps to forestall questioning on this point, he
declares that he has himself "examined their discourses and
investigated their books thoroughly, and they are all completely free of error." [53]

Jesuit teachings surpass the teachings of China's ancient
sages, Xu believes, by reaching deeper into the inner feelings of human beings, and thus guiding them to do good.
He offers an example from history: the early Chinese belief that there is no retribution for doing evil (he cites the
Han historian Sima Qian) has led men to practice deceit
and guile in order to avoid government restraints. "When
one law has been established, one hundred evil practices
have arisen," thus thwarting the desire for moral government. When Chinese turned to the Buddhist teaching of
retribution in another life, that too proved false, while Daoist
philosophy has been debased by superstition. By contrast,
the Jesuit teaching of "serving Heaven can truly enhance
the civilizing influence /of ancient rulers/, uphold and af-
firm the learning of the literati, and restore and correct the
laws of the Buddha." [54]

The appeal for Xu of the Jesuits' teachings on religion
and morality was enhanced by their knowledge of mathematics and the sciences. As a Confucian, Xu made no categorical distinction between these two spheres. In the petition defending missionaries in 1617, he urges the emperor
to permit officials of the imperial government to judge all
their writings — "what they say on serving Heaven and loving
man, on the investigation of things and pursuit of principle
to the utmost (*gewu qiongli*), on the art of ruling the empire,

on calendar calculation, on medical practice, on agriculture and water control"—and to punish him equally with the missionaries if any subversive teachings are found. [55] His preface to a treatise on water control (translated by Ricci and Li Zhizao in 1613) shows the same mixture of the moralistic and the practical. Although the subject is technology, he begins with a eulogy of Ricci's personal character. He also quotes from an ancient classic: "taking practical measures to bring profit to the empire is the greatest thing a sage can do." The word which he uses for sage (*shengren*) is the same as the Jesuits used for a Christian saint, showing that the missionaries had not clarified the differences between the two. [56]

Xu's confusion is understandable. Within the Confucian vision of a universal, self-perpetuating, organic universe there were no categories by which to distinguish "religious" from "scientific" modes of thought. *Religion* could be translated as *jiao* (guiding doctrine), or as *Dao* (the Way, or cosmic process). Both terms implied the guidance of man, and neither connoted supernatural influence. *Science,* on the other hand, had no equivalent term in Chinese that could embrace all the practical investigations in which Xu was engaged, except the highly general term *xue* (learning or study of natural or human affairs, usually from books). But *xue* also applied to the study of "religious" subjects such as the patterns of the cosmos (*Dao*) or the principle behind all phenomena (*li*). It is therefore unsurprising, as Gernet has noted, that many educated Chinese categorized all Jesuit writings under the single rubric of "heavenly studies" (*tianxue*), or sometimes as Western studies (*xixue*). [57]

Xu was drawn to mathematics, science, and technology by personal aptitude and childhood background. In the area around Shanghai where he grew up, handicraft technology was well developed and agriculture was enriched by water control techniques such as dredging, diking, and irrigation. There was doubtless much to intrigue a boy of mechanical inclination. Indeed, a letter about water control that he wrote to a Sanghai notable in 1603, before he had studied with Ricci, shows that his knowledge of practical mathematics had developed early. [50] As soon as he passed the final round of examinations in 1604, he is said to have abandoned further study of Confucian philosophy and turned to practical studies. [59]

In the Confucian world, however, practical studies constituted a moral endeavor, as is evident in Xu's views on mathematics. From 1604 to 1607 he worked closely with Ricci in Beijing and together they produced their translation of part of Euclid's *Principles of Geometry* (*Jihe yuanben*, in 6 *juan*, 1607). For Xu the publication represented the recovery of an early Chinese skill. Mathematics, he states, was an integral part of ancient Chinese intellectual life. It was one of the six arts of the Zhou period (the others were rites, music, archery, chariot driving, and writing) that were required for a man's moral education. Lost in the notorious burning of Confucian books by the first emperor of the Qin dynasty in 213 B.C., the application of mathematics since the Han dynasty (202 B.C.-220 A.D.) had been largely ineffective, "like a blind man shooting at a target, in vain and without results." [60] As mathematical training had made the men of antiquity superior to those of the present day, Xu believed, its revival could contribute to the moral improvement of his own time.

Xu applied this idea broadly. In a famous memorial late in his life (1630), he enumerated ten sub-areas of practical study that could be improved by the application of mathematics: climatic conditions, water control, musical tones, military technology, accounting, construction, mechanized power, topography, medicine, and horology. He described these fields as important to the welfare and the protection of the populace. [61] His own major achievements were in three areas, calendar reform, military technology and agricultural research. All reflect a Confucian's moral concern for the public weal.

An accurate calendar enabled the Chinese government to ascertain the seasons—essential for agriculture—and to predict celestial phenomena, notably solar and lunar eclipses, thus visibly confirming the emperor's mandate to rule the world "under Heaven." The Ming calendar, figured according to 365.25 days per year (an error of one day every 128 years), had not been rectified since the beginning of the dynasty. [62] The Bureau of Astronomy, as the Jesuits soon discovered, lacked the mathematical skills to institute a reform.[63] Several inaccuracies in eclipse prediction culminated in 1629 when the Bureau miscalculated a solar eclipse and Xu was appointed to supervise a calendar reform. Through his influence, a calendar bureau was organized with Jesuit missionaries in charge.[64] With their collaboration, he compiled a new calendar, published posthumously in 1635, which lasted until 1912.

Xu's military reforms were less successful, but also applied his mathematical and technological skills to his moral concern to protect the people. After a shattering defeat of Ming forces by the Manchus at Fushun in 1619, he sent up a series of memorials analyzing the disaster, proposing new tactics and advocating Western-style muskets and artillery. He personally trained a force of some 4,600 men which later compiled a record of successes in battle, he oversaw the manufacture of muskets in Beijing, and he arranged for the transportation of Western guns cast in Macao for the defense of northern cities. In these efforts he was frequently frustrated by corruption, incompetence, and vested interests, yet continued with patriotic persistence.[65]

Agriculture, like military defense, was a moral concern. In an age of commercial growth and urbanization, Xu embraced the traditional position that social order depended upon agrarian prosperity. The basic need of the age, he believed, was to "prohibit people from vagrancy and teach them to produce grain."[66] Xu's approach to the problem was more imaginative, more independent, and probably more "scientific" than any other thinker of his time. It combined extensive reading on agricultural techniques with experimental work in his private fields near Shanghai and Tianjin. To alleviate famine he tried out new plants (e.g. the sweet potato, recently introduced from the Americas). He introduced southern strains of rice in the northern climate. He experimented with fertilizers. He grew various kinds of trees (e.g. the tallow tree) seeking ways to increase their productivity. And he studied medicinal herbs. In his search for a way to fight locusts, he developed the hypothesis that they bred in the southern marshes as a kind of shrimp. Although incorrect, his conclusion was based on a careful analysis that included field research.[67] At the end of his life Xu assembled some of the major agricultural writings from the past together with his own work in an important compendium, *The Complete Book of Agricultural Administration* (*Nongzheng quanshu*). [68]

Xu pursued his work in these various fields of "practical studies" with the same moral commitment that he gave to his Christian faith. For him the Jesuits' teachings on scientific and even technological subjects confirmed their teachings on the Lord of Heaven. And all aspects of their work seemed to him consistent with the body of moral truth received from Chinese tradition.

Xu's career shows how, in the late Ming period, a Christian convert could serve a Confucian monarchy with honesty and conviction. In an age of uncertainty when effective government was breaking down and new social tensions were appearing, the Jesuits offered the promise of proven moral knowledge. That knowledge, both "religious" and "scientific," flowed in a broad cultural stream from a world where Christianity and science had not yet broken apart. For some Chinese, of whom Xu was one, it offered a coherent vision of a moral cosmos and a reformed social order, spiritually fulfilling and rationally convincing, where the ideals of the Confucian tradition itself might finally be realized.

With accommodation on one side and eclecticism on the other, Jesuit missionaries and their educated converts in late Ming China constructed a fragile bridge between their respective worlds. The blend of moral fervor and scientific practicality which the Jesuits brought from sixteenth-century Europe fitted well with the mixture of idealistic commitment and statecraft pragmatism that had developed among late Ming literati. In the end, however, Jesuit conversions in China were a transient achievement, nourished by compromise on both sides under circumstances which were historically unique. During the Qing dynasty (1644-1912), as the Jesuits' purposes became more fully understood, Chinese began to distinguish their teachings on Christianity from those on science and technology. [69] Under the Yong Zheng emperor (1722-1735) Christianity as a religion was proscribed altogether, and Jesuits were limited to services at the court primarily in their "scientific" capacities.

Notes

1. Joseph Dehergne, "Les Chrétientés de Chine de la Periode Ming (1581-1650)," *Monumenta Serica*, XVI (1957), 123.

2. *Ibid.*, p. 123.

3. *Ibid.*, p. 124.

4. Owen Chadwick, *The Reformation* (rev. ed.; Harmondsworth, Middlesex, England, 1972), pp. 257-262.

5. Donald F. Lach, *Asia in the Making of Europe*, I, *The Century of Discovery* (Chicago, 1965), 246.

6. *Ibid.*, pp. 279-280.

7. *Ibid.*, p. 50.

8. George Elison, *Deus Destroyed: The Image of Christianity in Early Modern Japan* (Cambridge, Mass., 1973), p. 57.

9. L. C. Goodrich (ed.), Chaoying Fang (assoc. ed.), *Dictionary of Ming Biography, 1368-1644* (New York, 1976), p. 1335. Hereafter cited as DMB.

10. Lach, *Century of Discovery*, p. 254.

11. Jonathan D. Spence, *The Memory Palace of Matteo Ricci* (New York, 1984), pp. 173-178.

12. Lach, *Century of Discovery*, pp. 800-801.

13. Spence, *Memory Palace...*, pp. 135-139.

14. DMB, p. 1142.

15. Kenneth K. S. Ch'en, "Matteo Ricci's Contribution to and Influence on Geographical Knowledge in China," *Journal of the American Oriental Society*, LIX (1939), 329-337.

16. John L. Mish, "Creating an Image of Europe for China: Aleni's *Hsi-fang ta-wen*, Introduction, Translation and Notes," *Monumenta Serica*, XXIII (1964), 43, 50, 61, 78.

17. David Landes, *Revolution in Time: Clocks and the Making of the Modern World* (Cambridge, Mass., 1983), p. 40.

18. A. R. Hall, *The Scientific Revolution, 1500-1800* (Boston, 1954), p. 104.

19. William L. Schurz, *The Manila Galleon* (New York, 1939, reprint, 1959), pp. 70, 81.

20. Susan Bush, *The Chinese Literati on Painting: Su Shih (1037-1101) to Tung Ch'i-ch'ang (1555-1636)* (Cambridge, Mass., 1971), pp. 156-157.

21. John B. Henderson, *The Development and Decline of Chinese Cosmology* (New York, 1984), p. 227.

22. Tileman Grimm, "Ming Education Intendants," in Charles O. Hucker

(ed.), *Chinese Government in Ming Times: Seven Studies* (New York, 1969), pp. 139, 146.

23. *Jiao Shi Danyuan xuji xu* /Preface to the Supplementary Collection of Jiao Hong's Works/, in Wang Zhongmin (ed.), *Xu Guangqi ji* /Collected Writings of Xu Guangqi/, 2 vols. (Beijing, 1963), I, 89. Hereafter cited as XGQJ.

24. DMB, pp. 1400, 1403.

25. Wolfgang Franke, *An Introduction to the Sources of Ming History* (Kuala Lumpur, 1968), p. 6; DMB, pp. 1059, 1190-1191.

26. Charles O. Hucker, "The Tung-lin Movement in the Late Ming Period," in John K. Fairbank (ed.), *Chinese Thought and Institutions* (Chicago, 1957), p. 141.

27. Joseph Needham, *Science and Civilization in China*, II (Cambridge, England, 1956), 493; Wing-tsit Chan (trans. and comp.), *A Source Book in Chinese Philosophy* (Princeton, 1963), p. 611.

28. Among the ways to search for principle, writes one, are to "read books and elucidate moral principles," to "discuss people and events of the past and present /and/ distinguish which are right and which wrong," and to "handle affairs and settle them in the proper way." Chu Hsi and Lu Tsu-ch'ien, *Reflections on Things at Hand, The Neo-Confucian Anthology*, Wing-tsit Chan (trans.) (New York, 1967), pp. 91-92.

29. Chan, *Source Book...*, p. 662.

30. Joanna F. Handlin, *Action in Late Ming Thought: The Reorientation of Lü K'un and Other Scholar-Officials* (Berkeley, 1983), pp. 194-195.

31. Heinrich Busch, "The Tung-lin shu-yuan and its Political and Philosophical Significance," *Monumenta Serica*, XIV (1949-1955), 47-48, 78-82; Hucker, "Tung-lin Movement...," pp. 143-147.

32. Yü Chun-fang, *The Renewal of Buddhism in China* (New York, 1981), pp. 65-66.

33. Wu Han, *Dushi zhaji* /Sundry Notes on Reading History/ (Beijing, 1956), pp. 24-25.

34. DMB, pp. 859-865.

35. DMB, pp. 368-369.

36. Liang Jiamian, *Xu Guangqi nianpu* /A Chronological Biography of Xu Guangqi/ (Shanghai, 1981), p. 53.

37. On Renaissance syncretism, see Henderson, *Development and Decline...*, pp. 40-41; on Lin Zhaoen, see DMB, pp. 913-915.

38. Hucker, "Tung-lin Movement...," p. 144; DMB, p. 816.

39. Yü, *Renewal of Buddhism...*, p. 4.

40. Biographical sketches of each are in Arthur W. Hummel (ed.), *Eminent Chinese of the Ch'ing Period (1644-1912)*, 2 vols. (Washington, DC, 1943).

41. Studies of his life are in Liang Jiamian, *Xu Guangqi...*; Lo Guang, *Xu*

Guangqi zhuan /A Biography of Xu Guangqi/ (Hong Kong, 1953); Monika Ubelhör, "Hsü Kuang-ch'i (1562-1633) und seine Einstellung zum Christentum," *Oriens Extremus*, XV, No. 2 (December, 1968), 191-257 and XVI, No. 1 (June, 1969), 41-74; and Joseph King-hap Ku, "Hsu Kuang-ch'i: Chinese Scientist and Christian (1562-1633)" (Ph.D. thesis, St. John's University, New York, 1973).

42. Lo Guang, *Xu Guangqi...*, p. 8 and notes on p. 11.

43. Jacques Gernet, *China and the Christian Impact* (Cambridge, England, 1985), p. 22.

44. See his biography in DMB, pp. 31-33.

45. *Ba erhshiwu yan* /Colophon to Twenty-five Sayings (from Epictetus)/, in XGQJ, p. 86.

46. XGQJ. p. 75.

47. Liang Jiamian, *Xu Guangqi...*, p. 69.

48. Nicola Trigault, *China in the Sixteenth Century*, trans. Louis J. Gallagher (New York, 1953), p. 451.

49. Lo Guang, *Xu Guangqi...*, p. 22.

50. See Handlin, *Action in Late Ming...*, pp. 208-212.

51. *Ba erhshiwu yan*, XGQJ, p. 87.

52. *Bianxue shugao* /Draft Petition of an Argument on (Christian) Teachings/ in Wu Xiangxiang (comp.), *Tianzhujiao dongchuan wenxian xubian* /Supplementary Edition of Documents on the Transmission of Catholicism to the East/ (Taipei, 1966), I, 22-23.

53. *Ibid.*, pp. 25-26. Xu does not mention such Christian mysteries as the Virgin birth, the Incarnation of Christ, or the redemption of man from sin. These were not stressed in early Jesuit writings, and I have found no evidence of his knowledge of them.

54. *Ibid.*, pp. 24-25.

55. *Ibid.*, p. 29.

56. *Taixi xuefa* /Western Hydraulic Methods/ in XGQJ, p. 67. On Jesuit problems with the word *saint*, see Gernet, *China and the Christian...*, pp. 158-159.

57. Gernet, *China and the Christian...*, p. 58.

58. Wang Zhongmin, preface to XGQJ, p. 5.

59. *Ibid.*, p. 7.

60. *Ke Jihe yuanben xu* /Preface to the *Jihe yuanben*/ in XGQJ, pp. 74-75.

61. XGQJ, pp. 337-338.

62. This was the same error as that in the Julian calendar, which by the fifteenth century had led to a discrepancy of 9 days between the vernal equinox and the calendar date of March 21, and brought on the Gregorian calendar reform.

63. Trigault, *China in the Sixteenth Century*, p. 329.

64. Liang Jiamian, *Xu Guangqi...*, pp. 163-166.

65. A summary of Xu's military work stressing his patriotism is given by his son, Xu Ji, in XGQJ, pp. 553-557; the memorials are on pp. 97-147. For the expeditions to bring Western guns to Beijing, see C. R. Boxer, "Portuguese Military Expeditions in Aid of the Mings against the Manchus." *T'ien Hsia Monthly*, VII, No. 8 (August, 1938), 24-33.

66. Quoted by Wan Guoding, "Xu Guangqi di xueshu luxian he dui nongye di gongxian" /Xu Guangqi's Academic Line and His Contribution to Agriculture/ in *Xu Guangqi jinian lunwen ji* /Commemorative Studies on Xu Guangqi), edited by the Section on the History of Chinese Natural Science of the Chinese Academy of Sciences (Beijing, 1963), p. 22.

67. See his *Chu huang* /On Exterminating Locusts/ in XGQJ, pp. 244-246.

68. Published after his death, it has recently gained new attention from Chinese historians. Reprinted as *Nongzheng quanshu jiaozhu*, with exegesis by Shi Shenghan, 3 vols. (Shanghai, 1979).

69. Gernet, *China and the Christian...*, p. 59.

Name Index

Antonio Acciaiuoli, Lord of Thebes (1394-1435) (d.1435).

Giulio Aleni (1582-1649), Italian Jesuit missionary; prolific writer of essays and tracts in Chinese.

Alexander the Great (356-323 B.C.), military conqueror and King of Macedonia (336-323 B.C.).

Pope Alexander V (pope 1409-1410) (d. 1410).

Paul Althaus (1888-1966), Evangelical-Lutheran theologian.

Francesco Amadi, Italian chronicler (d. 1566).

Emperor Andronikos III (emperor 1316-1341) (1291-1341).

Hannah Arendt (1906-1975), author of *Origins of Totalitarianism*.

Attila the Hun (d. 453), King of the Huns from 433.

James Baldwin (1924--), novelist, black American.

Karl Barth (1886-1968), Swiss Reformed theologian whose *Römerbrief* (1919) deeply stirred German intellectual and religious life; founder of a new orthodoxy, called "Dialectical Theology."

Yehuda Bauer (1926--), Israeli Holocaust historian.

Otto Baumgarten (1858-1934), liberal Evangelical-Protestant theologian, determined foe of anti-Semitism.

Bayezid, Ottoman Sultan (1389-1402) (d. 1403).

Pope Benedict XII (b. ca. 1285) (pope 1334-1342).

Peter Ludwig Berger (1929--), conservative sociologist, Boston University.

Hans Freiherr von Berlepsch (1843-1926), Prussian Minister of Commerce (1890-1896).

Bruno Bettelheim (1903--), contemporary Chicago psychoanalyst.

Otto von Bismarck (1815-1898), created the German Empire in 1871; chancellor until 1890.

Christoph Blumhardt (1842-1919), Swabian pastor who boldly endorsed socialism and became a Social Democrat.

Johann Christoph Blumhardt (1805-1880), Evangelical-Protestant pastor with strong convictions about realizing Christian identity through good works, sobriety and communal service.

Friedrich von Bodelschwingh (1831-1910), zealous missionary to the poor and downtrodden.

Dietrich Bonhoeffer (1906-1945), Evangelical-Protestant pastor and theologian; opposed the Third Reich and eventually suffered martyrdom.

Artur Bonus (1864-1941), a propagator of "Germanized Christianity."

Charles Booth (1840-1916), English philanthropist who subsidized massive statistical study (1891-1903) of London's poor and working class.

Boucicault, French Marshal (1366-1421).

Heinrich Brauns (1868-1939), Catholic priest, principal Center party expert on social issues.

Emil Brunner (1889-1966), Swiss Reformed theologian renowned for his clear exposition of "Dialectical Theology."

Friedrich Brunstäd (1883-1944), orthodox Lutheran theologian, active in the Evangelical-Social movement, headed its training school for social workers in Spandau (1922-1934).

The Buddha (ca. 500 B. C.), prince from northern India who became "The Enlightened One," the founder of Buddhism.

Domenico Cattaneo, Genoese Lord of Phokaia (ca. 1334-1335).

Lazare Cattaneo (1560-1640), Italian Jesuit; a pioneer of the China mission.

Houston Stewart Chamberlain (1855-1927), British-born political philosopher who publicized views on Aryan racial superiority; became a German citizen during World War I.

Christopher Clavius (1534-1612), German Jesuit mathematician; a leader in establishing the Gregorian calendar.

Pope Clement VI (pope 1342-1352) (1291-1352).

Pope Clement VII (b. ca. 1342), at Avignon (1378-1394).

Confucius (551-479 B.C.), Chinese teacher and philosopher.

Lucas Cranach (1472-1553), German painter.

Dante (1265-1321), Italian poet.

Joao da Rocha (1565-1623), Portuguese Jesuit; a pioneer of the China mission.

Angela Yvonne Davis (1944--), left-wing, black-American political activist.

Lucy Dawidowicz (1915--), Holocaust historian.

Fr. Iñigo de Alfaro, Hospital Captain of Smyrna (1402) (fl. 1400-1435).

Fr. Giovanni de Biandrate, Hospitaller Captain-General of Papal Fleet, 1344 (d. after 1351).

Ruy Gonçalez de Clavijo, Castilian envoy (d. 1412).

Shen Defu (1578-1642), historian; author of an important history of the Ming dynasty.

Fr. Dragonet de Joyeuse, Hospitaller (fl. 1337-1348).

Paul de Lagarde (1827-1892), German philosopher and philologist.

Hans Delbrück (1848-1929), German military historian.

Pico della Mirandola (1463-1494), Florentine humanist.

Fr. Raymond de Lescure, Prior of Toulouse (1396-1411) (d. 1411).

Pierre de Lusignan, King of Cyprus (king 1359-1369) (1329-1369).

Philippe de Mézières, Crusade propagandist (1327-1405).

Michel de Montaigne (1533-1592), French essayist.

Fr. Philibert de Naillac, Master of the Hospital (1396-1421) (d. 1421).

Anton de Quadros (fl. mid-16th century), Jesuit missionary; as Provincial of India (1559-1569), he shaped the Asian mission in its early years.

Jean de Nevers, Duke of Burgundy (duke 1404-1419) (1371-1419).

Rene Descartes (1596-1650), French mathematician and philosopher.

Fr. Foulques de Villaret (d. 1327), Master of the Hospitallers (1305-1319).

Otto Dibelius (1880-1967), Evangelical-Lutheran pastor; embodied a religious fervor for protecting the church from any form of modern totalitarian government.

Adolf Eichmann (1906-1975), bureaucratic linchpin in implementing Hitler's "final solution"; tried and executed in Israel.

Werner Elert (1885-1954), historian and systematic Lutheran theologian.

Queen Elizabeth I (r. 1558-1603), last Tudor monarch; presided over an era of cultural florescence in England.

Desiderius Erasmus (1469-1536), eminent Dutch humanist.

Matthias Erzberger (1875-1921), Center party leader (Roman Catholic); accepted the Versailles Treaty and energetically supported the Weimar Republic; assassinated by right-wing nationalists.

Euclid (fl. 300 B.C.), Greek mathematician whose *Elements* laid the foundation for geometry.

Emil L. Fackenheim (1916--), contemporary Holocaust theologian.

Helen Fein (1934--), author of *Accounting for Genocide*.

Henry Feingold (1931--), historian, City University of New York.

Erich Foerster (1865-1945), liberal Evangelical-Reformed theologian, closely associated with Martin Rade and *Christliche Welt*.

Johann Friedrich (1503-1554), Elector of Ernestine Saxony.

Emil Fuchs (b. 1874), Evangelical-Protestant pastor, a dedicated religious socialist.

Galileo Galilei (1564-1642), Florentine astronomer; pioneer in seventeenth-century science.

Jacopo Gattilusio, Lord of Lesbos (1403-1428) (d. 1428).

Erving Goffman (1922-1982), sociologist.

Friedrick Gogarten (b. 1887), Evangelical-Protestant theologian and philosopher; political conservative who believed that National Socialism represented God's continuous revelation in history.

Paul Göhre (1864-1928), Evangelical-Protestant pastor and Christian social activist with marked liberal tendencies.

William Josiah Goode (1917--) sociologist, student of praise and esteem.

Pope Gregory XI (pope 1370-1378) (1329-1378).

Xu Guangqi (1562-1633), Jesuit convert, scientist, and high official.

Adolf von Harnack (1851-1930), theologian and historian; led the Evangelical-Social Congress (1903-1911); defender of the Weimar Republic.

Gerhart Hauptmann (1862-1946), naturalistic dramatist who stirred German social consciousness.

Georg Wilhelm Friedrich Hegel (1770-1831), philosopher, influential German idealist.

Heinrich of Braunschweig-Wolfenbüttel (1489-1568), Duke of Braunschweig-Wolfenbüttel.

Henry IV, King of England (king 1399-1413) (1367-1413).

Theodor Herzl (1860-1904), founder of political Zionism (1897).

Paul von Hindenburg (1847-1934), German Field Marshall during World War I; elected President of the Weimar Republic in 1925; re-elected in 1932.

Georg Ernst Hinzpeter (1827-1907), from 1866-1879 tutor and companion to Prince William, the future William II.

Emanuel Hirsch (b. 1888), Evangelical-Lutheran theologian and historian; supported National Socialism to save Germany from Bolshevism.

Adolf Hitler (1889-1945), *Führer* of the Third Reich (1933-1945).

Adolf Hoffmann (1858-1930), bitterly anti-church Independent Social Democratic politician, alarming both German Protestants and Catholics during his brief tenure as Prussian Minister of Culture (1918-1919).

Karl Holl (1866-1926), Evangelical-Lutheran theologian and historical scholar whose works inaugurated the "Luther Renaissance."

Joachim Hossenfelder (1899--), Evangelical-Lutheran pastor, strove to establish a national "People's Church," taking National Socialism "on faith" and suppressing all the regional churches.

Yuan Huang (1533-1606), eclectic philosopher who authorized an important book an agriculture.

Victor Aimé Huber (1800-1869), German Protestant social reformer; sought to form Christian cooperative, self-help industrial communities.

Alfred Hugenberg (1865-1951), German press lord; gained control of the German National People's party and made it serve industrial interests; allied with Hitler and alienated many devout German Protestants from the party.

Ignatius of Smolensk, Russian traveller (fl. 1390).

Ilyas, Emir of Menteshe (1402-1421) (d. 1421).

Arthur James (Lord) Balfour (1848-1930), author of the "Balfour Declaration" (1917), legitimizing the idea of a Jewish homeland in the mandated territories.

Xu Ji (1582-1645), only son of Xu Guangqi; baptized a Christian.

Emperor John VI Kantakouzenos (emperor 1347-1354) (1293-1383).

Emperor John VII Palaeologus (b. 1370) (emperor 1399-1408) (d. 1408).

King John III (r. 1521-1557), Portuguese ruler; encouraged colonization abroad and supported the Jesuit Order.

Pope John XXIII (b. 1370) (pope 1410-1415) (d. 1419).

Junayd, usurper at Smyrna (d. ca. 1424).

Martin Kähler (1835-1912), profound theological scholar who synthesized major aspects of nineteenth-century Protestant theology.

Georgios Kalokires, Greek notary of the Hospital (fl. 1348).

Chaim Aaron Kaplan (c. 1880-1942), Warsaw ghetto diarist, murdered in the Holocaust.

Khizir, Overlord of the Emirate of Aidin and ruler of Ephesus (1334- ca. 1360) (d. ca. 1360).

Wilhelm Kube (1887-1943), radical German nationalist and anti-Semite; worked to subordinate the entire German Protestant ecclesiastical structure to the Third Reich.

Hermann Kutter (1869-1931), Swiss Reformed pastor, believed that social misery came from man's fall from God, whose restorative presence existed in the Social Democratic party.

Lao-Tzu (6th c. B.C.), mythical sage, venerated as author of a major classic of Daoism.

Vladimir Ilyich Lenin (1870-1924), principal leader of the Bolshevik faction that spearheaded the Russian Revolution (1917) and established the Soviet Union.

Theodor Lohmann (1831-1905), German public official and pious layman active in the Inner Mission.

Ignatius Loyola (1491-1556), Basque soldier and mystic; founder of the Society of Jesus (the Jesuit Order).

Erich Ludendorff (1865-1937), principal German military strategist during World War I; became a radical conservative and organized an eccentric cult based on the old Teutonic gods.

Ludolf of Sudheim, pilgrim (fl. 1340).

Martin Luther (1483-1546), German religious reformer, theologian, and Protestant reformer.

Emperor Manuel II (emperor 1373-1421) (1350-1421).

Masud, Emir of Menteshe (d. probably before 1319).

Wilhelm Maurer (1900--), Professor, University of Erlangen.

Prince Max of Baden (1867-1929), the last effective German Chancellor (October 3 - November 9, 1918).

Henry Mayhew (1812-1887), English journalist who made pioneering studies of London's laboring poor.

Mehmet, Ottoman Sultan (1402-1421) (d. 1421).

Philip Melanchthon (1497-1560), Professor of Greek and Protestant reformer.

Yehudi Menuhin (1916--), violinist; anti-Zionist.

John Milton (1608-1674), English poet.

George Mosse (1918--), historian, University of Wisconsin.

Lewis Mumford (1895--), known for utopian urban theory in 1920s-1940s.

Reinhard Mumm (1873-1932), Evangelical-Lutheran pastor; German National party Reichstag deputy who supported social legislation.

Musa, Ottoman Sultan (1402-1413) (d. 1413).

Friedrich Naumann (1860-1919), Evangelical-Protestant social reformer with liberal theological and political views.

Jacob Neusner (1932--), Director of Jewish Studies Program, Brown University; historian and historicist of canonical Jewish texts.

Nikephoros Gregoras, Byzantine historian (d. 1359).

Niquita of Assiza, Syrian at Rhodes (fl. 1400).

Marcel Ophuls (1927--), director of French film, "The Sorrow and the Pity."

Orhkan, son of Masud, Emir of Menteshe (ca. 1319--1333/1337) (d. 1333/1337).

Orhkan, son of Osman, Ottoman ruler (1326-1362).

Cynthia Ozick (1928--), contemporary novelist and allegorist.

Talcott Parsons (1902-1979), Harvard sociologist, founder of "Structural Functionalism."

Philip IV, King of France (1268-1314) (king 1285-1314).

Pius IX (1792-1878), pope from 1846, opposed modern trends in politics and theology; extreme ultramontanist.

Leon Poliakov (1910--), French historian of anti-Semitism.

Arthur Graf von Posadowsky-Wehner (1845-1932), Reichs Minister of the Interior (1897-1907).

Sima Qian (d. ca. 85 B.C.), eminent Han dynasty historian.

Martin Rade (1857-1940), liberal Protestant theologian and social-political reformer.

Leonhard Ragaz (1868-1945), Swiss Reformed pastor, identified God's·revelation in the Swiss Social Democratic party.

Leopold von Ranke (1795-1866), historian, founder of the modern German historical school.

Ernst von Rath (--1938), Third Secretary of the German Embassy in Paris.

Matteo Ricci (1551-1610), Italian Jesuit missionary; pioneered the Jesuit mission in China.

Jacob Riis (1849-1914), American journalist who exposed the vast scale of urban poverty.

Albrecht Ritschl (1822-1889), German Protestant theologian of late nineteenth century who inspired Evangelical social reformers.

Jacob Robinson (1889--), author of *The Crooked Shall Be Made Straight*, an attack on Hannah Arendt's *Eichmann in Jerusalem*.

Paul A. Robinson (1940--), author.

Albrecht Count von Roon (1803-1879), Prussian general and War Minister (1859-1873), initiated the rebuilding of the Prussian army.

Hans Rothfels (1891--) German-born historian, emigrated to U.S.A.

Richard Lowell Rubenstein (1924--), Holocaust commentator.

Michele Ruggieri (1543-1607), Italian Jesuit; together with Matteo Ricci, established the first post-medieval Christian mission in China.

Saladin, Sultan of Egypt (1174-1193) (d. 1193).

Niccolò Sanudo, Venetian Duke of Naxos (1323-1341) (d. 1341).

Martin Sasse, Lutheran Bishop of Thuringia (1934-1941).

Adolf Schlatter (1852-1938), Evangelical-Protestant theologian.

Friedrich Ernst Daniel Schleiermacher (1768-1834), German theologian; stressed religious experience as basis for faith and doctrine.

Gustav Schmoller (1838-1917), German historical economist.

Fr. Albert von Schwarzburg (fl. 1312-1329; died after 1329).

Reinhold Seeberg (1859-1935), Evangelical-Lutheran theologian whose popular writing contributed to a closer identification of Protestantism and German nationalism.

William Shakespeare (1564-1616), English poet and dramatist, English playwright.

Li Shizhen (1518-1593), naturalist and pharmacologist; compiler of China's most important pharmacopoeia.

Wang Shizhen (1526-1590), man of letters; a leader in a movement to return to classical styles in literature.

Sigismund, King of Hungary (king 1385-1437) (1361-1437).

Rudolf Sohm (1841-1917), jurist and scholar of Roman and canon law; held that the Christian church was invisible, so that, for Protestants, only the political authority was legitimate.

Soloman, Syrian at Rhodes (fl. 1290-1320).

Friedrich Julius Stahl (1802-1861), conservative philosopher of law and the state; sustained a conservative political theology.

Wilhelm Stapel (1882-1954), Evangelical-Lutheran theologian, began in the 1920s to develop a radical concept of the Peoples' Church (*Volkskirche*) as the spiritual core of an authoritarian nation-state.

Adam Stegerwald (1874-1945), Catholic trade union organizer.

Adolf Stoecker (1835-1909), Court Chaplain who took Protestant social reform issues into politics; anti-Semitic.

Gustav Stresemann (1878-1929), Chancellor (1923) and

Foreign Minister (1923, 1924-1929) of the Weimar Republic; a liberal Protestant.

Carl Freiherr von Stumm-Halberg (1836-1901), Saar industrialist, reactionary "chimney baron" hostile to social reform legislation.

William Styron (1925--), novelist, author of *Sophie's Choice.*

Suleyman, Ottoman Sultan (1402-1411) (d. 1411).

Theodore, Despot of Morea (despot 1380-1407) (ca. 1350-1407).

Paul Tillich (1886-1965), Evangelical-Protestant theologian and philosopher; sought to bridge the gap (opened up by Barth's "Dialectical Theology") between supernaturalism and all the spheres of human thought and effort.

Timur, Turkic Khan (1369-1405) (ca. 1336-1405).

Yang Tingyun (1557-1627), Jesuit convert, official, and scholar.

Alfred von Tirpitz (1849-1930), German admiral and State Secretary of the Navy (1898 ff.).

Ferdnand Tönnies (1855-1936), German sociologist.

Marino Sanudo Torsello, Venetian publicist (d. 1337).

Ernst Troeltsch (1865-1923), German historian and sociologist; showed that Christian churches invariably accommodated the secular world (*The Social Teaching of the Christian Churches*, 1912).

Umur, Emir of Aidin (d. 1348) (emir 1334-1348).

Pope Urban VI (pope 1362-1370 (1310-1370).

Allesandro Valignano (1539-1606), Superior of all Jesuit missionary enterprises in India and East Asia; initiated Jesuit policy of cultural accommodation.

Giovanni Villani, Florentine chronicler (d. 1348).

Hermann Wagener (1815-1889), conservative journalist and politician; advised Bismarck on social issues.

Adolf Wagner (1835-1917), historical economist critical of laissez faire.

Michael Walzer (1935--), political scientist, Institute for Advanced Studies, Princeton.

Ludwig Weber (1846-1922), Evangelical-Lutheran pastor closely associated with Adolf Stoecker.

Max Weber (1864-1920), German sociologist and historian.

Chaim Weizmann (1874-1952), East European Jewish chemist who lobbied the English for Zionism; Israel's first president.

Johann Heinrich Wichern (1808-1881), founder of the Inner Mission; laid the basis for Protestant Christian social effort in Germany.

William I (1797-1888), King of Prussia (1861-1888).

William II (1859-1941), King of Prussia and German Emperor (1888-1918).

Georg Wünsch (1887-1964), Evangelical-Lutheran theologian.

Michael Wyschograd (1928--), philosopher, City University of New York.

Francis Xavier (1506-1552), Jesuit missionary, first to introduce Christianity to China.

Zhu Xi (1130-1200), eminent philosopher; an architect of neo-Confucianism.

Wang Yangming (1472-1529), philosopher; developed a major school of philosophy within the neo-Confucian tradition.

Zhu Yijun, the Wanli Emperor (e. 1573-1620), Chinese emperor whose long reign witnessed a distinct weakening of the Ming dynasty.

Yin-chen, the Yong Zheng emperor (r. 1722-1735), Manchu emperor, known for his autocratic rule.

Martino Zaccaria (d. 1345), co-lord of Chios (1314-1319).

Zhu Zaiyu (1536-1611), scholar and mathematician; did important work on the Chinese calendar.

Lin Zhaoen (1517-1598), religious leader; propagated the essential oneness of the three religions: Confucianism, Daoism and Buddhism.

Li Zhi (1527-1602), eclectic scholar; outspoken critic of neo-Confucianism.

Li-Zhizao (1565-1630), Jesuit convert, mathematician, and official.

Mei Zu (fl. ca. 1510-1543), historian; famous for detecting forgeries in ancient classics.

List of Contributors

Mark U. Edwards Jr. has been Professor of History at Purdue University; he is now at the Divinity School, Harvard University. Among his major publications are *Luther and the False Brethren* (Stanford, 1975), and *Luther's Last Battles*: *Politics and Polemics, 1531-1546* (Ithaca, New York, 1983).

William O. Shanahan is Professor of History at Hunter College and the Graduate School and University Center of the City University of New York. He has published widely on the history of Germany. His books include *Prussian Military Reforms, 1786-1813* (New York and London, 1945) and *German Protestants Face the Social Question* (Notre Dame, Indiana, 1954).

John Murray Cuddihy is Professor of Sociology at Hunter College of the City University of New York. Among his publications are *The Ordeal of Civility*: *Freud, Marx, Levi-Strauss and the Jewish Struggle with Modernity* (New York, 1974) and *No Offense*: *Civil Religion and Protestant Taste* (New York, 1978).

Dr. Anthony Luttrell has lectured and taught at many colleges and universities. He was recently a Visiting Member of the School of Historical Studies at the Institute for Advanced Study at Princeton and previously a fellow at the Harvard University Center for Byzantine Studies, Dumbarton Oaks, Washington, DC. His many publications include *The*

Hospitallers in Cyprus, Rhodes, Greece and the West, 1291-1440: Collected Studies (London, 1978) and *Latin Greece, the Hospitallers and the Crusades, 1291-1440: Collected Studies* (London, 1982).

Charlton M. Lewis is currently Professor and Chairman of the Department of History at Brooklyn College of the City University of New York. Professor Lewis is the author of *Prologue to the Chinese Revolution: The Transformation of Ideas and Institutions in Hunan Province, 1891-1907* (Cambridge, Mass., and London, 1976).

DATE DUE
